Soul Food
Lessons from Hearth to Heart

Dene Ward

Soul Food: Lessons from Hearth to Heart
© 2012 by DeWard Publishing Company, Ltd.
P.O. Box 6259, Chillicothe, Ohio 45601
800.300.9778
www.deward.com

Cover design by Jonathan Hardin.

The preponderance of Bible quotations are taken from the American Standard Version. Any emphasis in Bible quotations is added.

Reasonable care has been taken to trace original sources for any excerpts and quotations appearing in this book and to document such information. For material not in the public domain, fair-use standards and practices were followed. Should any attribution be found to be incorrect or incomplete, the publisher welcomes written documentation supporting correction for subsequent printings.

Printed in the United States of America.

ISBN: 978-1-936341-33-7

For two little boys who licked beaters, cut out pie crust hand prints, and regularly pilfered the cookie jar…

And for a new one I hope will do the same.

Better is a little with the fear of the LORD than great treasure and trouble with it. Better is a dinner of herbs where love is than a fattened ox and hatred with it. (Prov 15.16–17)

Preface

A few years ago I started writing email devotionals. Due to a serious eye condition, many of my other opportunities to serve had been taken away from me so this seemed like a good way to help others despite the many days I was confined to my home. It eventually led to the publication of *Flight Paths*, a devotional book designed to take the reader through every day for a year with an essay and appropriate spiritual application.

Lately several readers have asked for "another collection." Others have asked for smaller books to give as hostess gifts, to tuck into wedding shower presents, or welcome-to-the-neighborhood baskets. Since I am at least 150 articles away from another book of 366, I began looking through the ones I had filed away and discovered that many fall neatly into several different categories—bird watching, camping, gardening, the music studio, home and family, and the one that had the most in it—the kitchen. So here is the first of what should be several smaller books, just as so many have requested.

In choosing them, I wanted as many new ones as possible, but I found older ones from *Flight Paths* that had brought so much feedback, or evoked so many memories from the past—particularly of little boys who came running the moment they heard the mixer start—that I had to include some of them as well. But I promise more than half of these are brand new, never having appeared in a printed book before. We settled on 52—one a week for a year if you wish to use it that way.

I grew up in a house where it seems like we were always feeding someone. A table full of college students for a home-cooked Sunday dinner, a house full of church family singing hymns until they became too hoarse to croak and then snacking the rest of the evening away, neighbors solving the world's problems over coffee and cake, a room full of women laughing and chatting through a bridal shower, plus all the various girlfriends and boyfriends I was never embarrassed to bring home with me. I knew they would be fed, and fed well.

I am not a gourmet cook, I just enjoy cooking, and trying things I have never even heard of before. I am, though, an unabashed and unashamed *Southern* cook—some dishes have to be a certain way or they are just not right.

I have fed my share of school pals, girlfriends, visiting preachers, neighbors, church folks, and occasionally people I had never met before they knocked on my door that day. I have always tried to offer them a nourishing meal, just as I offer now this collection to feed your souls, lessons from my hearth to your heart.

Dene Ward

Soul Food

1. The Kitchen Floor

The kitchen must be the favorite room in nearly every home. It's where the family meets to share their meals and their day, to gather important information—"Mom! Where are my good jeans?"—to pick up sustenance when the time between meals is long and the activities vigorous, and a place for sharing thoughts, dreams, and childhood troubles over chocolate chip cookies and ice cold milk. When the kitchen is full of people and laughter, all is right with the world.

That makes the kitchen floor a microcosm of how we all live. All you have to do is drop something small, something that requires your face to be an inch above the floor trying to spy the odd shape or color, and suddenly you know everything anyone has eaten, spilled, or tracked in, even if you clean your floor regularly. If I had every dustpan full of sweepings over my 38 years of marriage, it would make a ten foot high pile of sugar granules, flour, cornmeal, panko, cookie crumbs, Cheerios, oats, blueberries, chopped parsley, basil, rosemary, the papery skins of onions and garlic cloves, freshly ground coffee beans, tiny, stray low dose aspirins, grains of driveway sand, clumps of garden soil, yellow clay, limerock, soot, burnt wood, strands of hair from blonde to nearly black to gray and white, frayed threads, missing buttons, assorted screws, and loose snips from the edges of coupons. If I had never cleaned the floor at all, it would be layered with coffee drips, dried splashes of dishwater, bacon grease and olive oil splatter, tea stains, grape juice, and sticky spots from honey and molasses spills while I was baking.

Put it all together and you would have a pretty good idea how we live our lives.

Every soul has a kitchen floor, places where the accumulated spills of life gather. We must regularly clean that floor, just as I am constantly sweeping and wiping and mopping, trying to stay ahead of the messes we make. As soon as I miss a day or a week, I have even more to clean up. It would be ridiculous to think I could ignore that floor and no one would know about us, wouldn't it?

Jesus said, "Out of the abundance of the heart the mouth speaks" (Matt 12.34). You can deny it all you want, but what you speak shows who you really are. I can say I never bake, but whoever sweeps my floor will know better. I can pretend we don't like Italian cuisine, but the evidence is right there. I can tell everyone we live in the city instead of the country, but the soil on my floor will say otherwise. It is getting harder for me to see those things now and to sweep them up perfectly, but my blindness to them will not keep others from knowing exactly what I do here all day long.

That kitchen floor of a heart will tell on you too. All you have to do is open your mouth. If you don't keep it cleaned up, if you don't monitor the things you store in it, it could belie your protestations of a righteous life. Sooner or later a word will slip out, a thought will take root and become a spoken idea. I heard someone say once that you cannot imagine in others what is not already in your own heart.

Of course, what's on your floor could prove your righteous life instead of denying it. So take a moment today to examine your kitchen floor. Let it remind you to examine your heart as well. I had much rather people see sugar and cookie crumbs than Satan's muddy footprints.

Let the words of my mouth and the meditation of my heart be acceptable in your sight, O Lord, my rock and my redeemer.

Psalm 19.14

2. Refrigerator Shelves

A few days ago, I used up several items at once that normally sit on the bottom shelf of the refrigerator door—the cranberry juice, the ketchup, and the mustard. Suddenly a third of that shelf was bare and I was horrified. How in the world did it ever get that dirty?

I pulled out the mayonnaise, the tahini, the Worcestershire and soy sauces, the maple syrup, the sesame seed oil, and the hoisin and was even more appalled. Black rings, sticky smears, and brown drops covered the narrow plastic ledge. I always wipe things off before I put them up, don't I? Well, maybe not always. Sometimes I'm in a hurry, sometimes my hands are full, sometimes I leave the putting up for someone else. Needless to say, I cleaned that shelf immediately, and the next day the whole refrigerator.

That sort of thing happens far more often than we like to think and in far more important places than refrigerators. Relationships come to mind.

I think wedding anniversaries are important, and not because I am a woman with unrealistic expectations. We have never been able to afford expensive gifts or excursions. Most often we stay at home and have a quiet dinner together. Sometimes it isn't even on the same day as our anniversary. A long time ago we stopped making the calendar our taskmaster. We celebrate birthdays on weekends, and holidays around work schedules. We have even celebrated our mid-June anniversary in July.

No, the thing about anniversaries is the re-connecting. You talk, you remember, you plan. You remind yourselves why you wound up together in the first place, and the place you want to eventually wind up together for eternity. In doing so every year, or even more often, you get that shelf cleaned up before the stains have a chance to set, before the caked on residue of life builds to the point that only a hard, painful scrub can remove it.

The same thing can happen among brethren. Why do you think God expects us to go to one another instead of letting things fester? Most problems between good-hearted people are simple misunderstandings that can be cleaned up with a quick wipe. You only need harsh abrasives when you let them sit awhile.

When was the last time you checked your relationship with your God? The last time you talked to him? The last time you let him speak to you by opening his Word? When was the last time that communication actually effected a change in you? When did you alter plans for the day or the attitude you presented to your family, or friends, or even perfect strangers because of your relationship with God? Maybe the grunge on your shelf has gotten too thick to penetrate.

Pay attention to the things you seldom think to look at, the things you take for granted. Wipe off your shelves once in a while, whether you think they need it or not.

Who shall ascend the hill of the LORD? And who shall stand in his holy place? He who has clean hands and a pure heart, who does not lift up his soul to what is false and does not swear deceitfully. He will receive blessing from the LORD and righteousness from the God of his salvation.

Psalm 24.3–5

3. Where Are the Cookies?

Several years ago, a prominent female politician angered many American women when she answered a reporter about her choice of career over homemaking by saying, "Well I suppose I could have stayed home and *baked cookies.*" Most of us read a sneer in her tone and, as I remember it, her office was inundated with homemade cookies baked and sent by outraged homemakers.

One of the things I decided to do as a homemaker was to keep a cookie jar filled with homemade cookies, and for the most part I have. Chewy oatmeal raisin, spicy gingersnaps, crumbly peanut butter, sparkly snickerdoodles, decadent triple chocolate, wonderful almond crunch cookies that always surprise people and steal the show, and all those variations of the All-American chocolate chip: Toll House, Neimann Marcus, peanut butter chocolate chip, double chocolate chip, oatmeal chocolate chip, and death by chocolate chocolate chip. My boys would come home from their friends' houses talking about how deprived they were—all they had were Oreos.

My younger son Nathan was especially fond of cookies. As a toddler, he would pull up a chair to stand in so he could "help" me make cookies—help that usually involved tasting the dough to make sure it was good, and then "cleaning" the beaters. When he was in high school, I bought him a shirt that said, *The Big Questions: Who Am I? Why Am I Here? What is my fate? WHERE ARE THE COOKIES?*

Eventually that chubby, tow-headed, blue-eyed cherub became a long, lean man who went off to college. The first time he came home he brought a friend with him. He immediately led the buddy to the counter where the cookie jar always sat. "See? I *told* you there would be cookies." Until he married I would bake cookies and save a dozen each week in a freezer bag until I had four or five kinds, then mail them to him and start all over. This was one serious cookie connoisseur. I am not sure what else made an impression on him, but I know he will remember that I loved him enough to make cookies for him.

I am reminded of David after his small army defeated the Amalekites. Not all of his men were as righteous as he. Several "wicked men and base fellows" did not want to share the spoils with the men who had stayed at camp, guarding their belongings. David said, "You shall not do so, my brothers, with that which Jehovah has given us... the share of him who goes down to the battle shall be the same as he who tarried by the baggage; they shall share alike, and it was from that day forward a statute and ordinance in Israel" (1 Sam 30.23–25). David understood the value of those who did the behind-the-scenes work, the jobs others considered less important, and which seldom received glory or recognition.

Think about Dorcas. Stephen, the deacon and great preacher, had been killed not long before. James the apostle, a cousin of Jesus himself, would be next. But who did Peter raise from the dead? Not the powerful speakers who performed miracles, but a widow who made clothes for the poor (Acts 9.36–42). Surely *God* was saying that what we consider small and unimportant tasks are actually some of the greatest of all.

Never underestimate the importance of baking cookies.

For whosoever shall give you a cup of water to drink because you are Christ's, truly I say to you, he shall not lose his reward.

Mark 9.41

4. Fat Free Living

I accidentally made some healthy cookies a few weeks ago. I had not taken the time to pick up my glasses and the magnifying glass. I had just concentrated hard and was sure the recipe said, "1 ½ sticks of butter." After the cookies came out of the oven, I was disappointed in their dry, cakey texture, when I had expected something chewy and rich. So I picked up my glasses and looked again—"1 ½ *cups* of butter." That is three whole sticks. What I had done was cut the butter in half. Low fat cookies were not what I had in mind, but it did help to say to myself, "For low fat, they're not that bad."

As Christians we often focus so often on what we cannot do—all those "thou shalt nots"—that it is amazing we can endure. Our faith becomes negative instead of positive. It is all about what we do not do, not what we do. That may explain why so many of us are bitter and why we never manage to spread the good news—to us it isn't such good news.

It also explains why we lose so many of our children. Your home should be a place of safety, a place of contentment, a place of love and laughter. It should be a haven for your children and their friends. Do you want to know where they are, what they are doing, and with whom? Make your home a pleasant place to be, not a prison they hope to break out of someday, and you will know where they are, because *home* is where they are, and where they want to be.

Christians should be known for what they do, not for what they don't do, for who they are, not who they aren't. If your friends were asked to describe Christians based on their knowledge of you, what would they say? "Christians are people who don't drink, who don't gamble, who don't go to clubs, who don't curse, who don't engage in non-marital sex, who don't smoke or take drugs, who don't watch certain movies and TV shows," and on and on. Or would they say, "Christians are happy, generous people who help others whenever a need arises, who are always having people in their homes—you can hear the laughter going on all evening. They are honest and forgiving. You know you can trust them because you never hear them gossip. They are pleasant to be around and seem to be able to handle anything life throws at them, and handle it well. They are the best people on earth. I wish I was more like them."

God has always promised his people "fat" lives. He told the Israelites they would have "a land flowing with milk and honey (Exod 3.8). When Nehemiah brought them back from captivity, he reminded them that they had taken "fortified cities, and a fat land, and possessed houses full of all good things, cisterns hewn out, vineyards, and oliveyards, and fruit-trees in abundance: so they did eat, and were filled, and became fat, and delighted themselves in [God's] great goodness" (9.25). But they focused only on the restraints of righteous living instead of the blessings, finally fell away to the heathens whose lives they envied, and God sent them away to punishment.

Yet still, He had Ezekiel tell them of another good land, a Messianic kingdom that would bring joy and peace. "And I will bring them out from the peoples, and gather them from the countries, and will bring them into their own land; and I will feed them upon the mountains of Israel, by the watercourses, and in all the inhabited places of the country. I will feed them with good pasture; and upon the mountains of the height of Israel shall their fold be: there shall they lie down in a good fold; and on fat pasture shall they feed upon the mountains of Israel" (34.13–14). That is exactly where we find ourselves today, in that "fat" Messianic kingdom, so why do we so often insist that the life of a Christian is a miserable one?

God has never required "fat-free living;" in fact, He has promised just the opposite. Concentrate today on the peace that living as a child of God brings to your life. Focus on the joy of salvation and the fellowship of a spiritual family. Contemplate the good in your life. The rest of the world deals with addictions, legal problems, disrupted families, purposeless lives, and finally, illness and death without hope and comfort. Talk about a negative life.

Go out and enjoy the fat in your life today.

The thief comes not, but that he may steal, and kill, and destroy: I came that they may have life, and may have it abundantly.

John 10.10

5. Filling

I do not understand the recent fascination with cupcakes. To me a special cake is huge, having three layers, interesting ingredients that make it moist and flavorful, and a filling as well as a frosting. Then I found a recipe for dark chocolate cupcakes with chocolate ganache filling, and a sour cream chocolate frosting. Okay, I thought, maybe these cupcakes are worth eating.

I spent two afternoons working on these things, two wasted afternoons as it turns out. Something happened to my chocolate ganache filling, and I still don't know what it was. Maybe I stubbed my toe when I measured the heavy cream and got a half teaspoon too much. Maybe I crossed my eyes when I weighed the chocolate and used half an ounce too little. Whatever it was, it ruined the cupcakes. The picture showed a cupcake cut in half with a rich, creamy filling clearly visible. Mine had a hole in the center where the filling was supposed to have been. True, your taste buds could tell something else had once been there, but it was not there any longer, and we couldn't find it anywhere. It had simply disappeared, leaving me with just another cupcake, and I was supremely disappointed.

I wonder if God does not sometimes feel the same about us. Yes, we must live in a world of sin and evil and hatred and all sorts of villainy. But He expects us to stand untainted, obviously different than those around us. Too often we just melt into the crowd. Maybe you could tell we had once been there—maybe someone remembers a person who was a little different than everyone else, but if he can no longer be found, how long will that influence last? Someone who disappears so easily will not be remembered long.

We are the sweet filling in the middle of a sinful world. We should be plainly visible. We should make the world a better place to live. Everyone should be scrambling to get to the good stuff—us! Our speech, our actions, our forgiving nature and calming influence, the fact that we actually stand for something and stand firm in it, rather than going along with the popular notions of right and wrong which change with the seasons—those things ought to make us easy to see, not easily camouflaged.

Make sure you stand out. Make sure you don't become part of an amalgamation that makes you just another face in the crowd, a hole where something special used to be.

So then, my beloved, even as you have always obeyed, not as in my presence only, but now much more in my absence, work out your own salvation with fear and trembling, for it is God who works in you both to will and to work, for his good pleasure. Do all things without murmurings and questionings; that you may become blameless and harmless, children of God without blemish in the midst of a crooked and perverse generation, among whom you are seen as lights in the world, holding forth the word of life.

Philippians 2.12–16

6. Lemon Juice

Do you know that it is practically impossible to find plain old banana ice cream in the grocery store? You can find banana split ice cream and banana cream pie ice cream, but not plain banana. So overripe bananas were on sale a few weeks ago and Keith bought some to make ice cream. As we were in the middle of mashing bananas I added a splash of lemon juice and suddenly we were having a conversation about it. He was just sure I had ruined his banana ice cream and made it sour—why the whole thing would curdle now, didn't I know that?

The past few weeks he has started watching me do things and asking questions for the inevitable day when he will need to take over. In the past, he has never known that I add a splash of lemon juice to a lot of things, his favorite apple pie, his favorite blueberry crisp, his favorite peach cobbler, his favorite crab cakes, and I could go on and on. Lemon juice is one of those things that brighten flavors and make things taste better, even though you don't actually taste the lemon—similar to salt in baked goods. Any good cook knows that if you leave the salt out of the cookies or the cake or the pie crust or the biscuits, none of them will be fit to eat. You don't know it is in there, but you sure know it if it isn't.

I have a feeling we treat God's blessings that way sometimes. We never really notice all the good things we have, but I bet if they suddenly disappeared we would. Oh yes, we often thank God for the really big things like salvation and grace, but what if you got up to a black and white world tomorrow morning?

Have you ever really thought about the blessing of color? We thank God every day for the food on our tables, but what if suddenly you could no longer taste it? Let me tell you, I have had that problem with these eye medications and it is awful. About the only thing good about it was a ten pound weight loss in two weeks, but there comes a point when even that is not a blessing.

You see, God is responsible for everything good, even the seemingly small, unimportant things. When your life takes a turn for the worse, it is easy to forget that and blame God. But by remembering that there are still good things, like color and taste, like flowers and butterflies, like puppies and kittens, like rain on the roof and a breeze in the trees, like a *real* vine-ripened tomato, you can know that God is still there, he is still giving you blessings. They may be blessings like lemon juice in banana ice cream or salt in cookies: just because you don't notice them, doesn't mean He doesn't care.

> *You visit the earth and water it, you greatly enrich it; the river of God is full of water. You provide their grain for so you have prepared it. You water its furrows abundantly, settling its ridges, softening it with showers and blessing its growth. You crown the year with your bounty, your wagon tracks overflow with abundance. The pastures of the wilderness overflow, the hills gird themselves with joy, the meadows clothe themselves with flocks, the valleys deck themselves with grain; they shout and sing together for joy.*
>
> Psalm 65.9–13

7. Coconut Cream Pie

Many years ago we were in a discussion with a group of Christians about the word "temptation" when Keith mentioned that "tempt" by its very definition means a possibility of and a desire to give in to that temptation. No one wanted to accept that statement, probably because we all want to believe that we don't want to sin. We happened to know a certain brother's dessert preferences because we had often eaten with that couple, and suddenly the solution came to me.

"Bill cannot be tempted off his diet by a coconut cream pie," I said. "He cannot be tempted that way because he hates coconut. Maybe chocolate, but not coconut." Click! The light bulb went on for practically everyone. Suddenly they understood what it meant to be tempted.

That understanding can lead to all sorts of discussions and get you into some deep water, but consider this one thing with me this morning. I was "raised in the church," as we often put it. I had parents who taught me right from wrong in no uncertain terms. Frankly, I have never even been tempted by most of the "moral" sins out there in the world. I know a lot of others in the same situation. But that doesn't make us any better than someone who has just recently given his life to the Lord. I am afraid that sometimes we think it does make us better. When a young Christian tells me that older Christians look down on him when he says he still struggles with sin, I *know* we think so.

Yet how does the fact that you have never struggled with a certain sin make you stronger than one who does? In fact, since you have never struggled with it, how do you know you could win the fight at all? There may be other temptations that cause us to fall, and not needing to fight one doesn't mean we would be any better at fighting others.

It only shows how weak we are when we pride ourselves on the fact that we have never been tempted in certain areas. Ironically, that very feeling *is* our weakness, the thing that tempts us, and the thing in which we usually fail—pride, self-righteousness, unjust judgment, and a failure to love as we ought.

What is your coconut cream pie? What distaste keeps you from even being tempted in one area, and as a result, makes you fail the test of humility? I might have to have a piece of pie while I think about it.

> *And he spoke also this parable unto certain who trusted in themselves that they were righteous, and set all others at nought: Two men went up into the temple to pray; the one a Pharisee, and the other a publican. The Pharisee stood and prayed thus with himself, God, I thank you, that I am not as the rest of men, extortioners, unjust, adulterers, or even as this publican. I fast twice in the week; I give tithes of all that I get. But the publican, standing afar off, would not lift up so much as his eyes unto heaven, but smote his breast, saying, God, be merciful to me a sinner. I say unto you, This man went down to his house justified rather than the other: for every one that exalts himself shall be humbled; but he that humbles himself shall be exalted.*
>
> Luke 18.9–14

8. A Biscuit Recipe

A young woman is making biscuits for her new husband. When she tries to roll them out she has a problem—they keep falling apart. It is all she can do to make them stick together long enough to get them on the baking sheet. And when she tries to take them off, they fall to pieces. Her husband tells her, "That's all right. It's the taste that matters," as he gallantly takes a bite, and a little bite is all he can get. They crumble so easily he cannot even butter them. Before long, his plate is filled with crumbs and he has not managed to eat even half a biscuit's worth.

The next morning she calls her mother. "Too much shortening," her mother says. So that evening the new bride tries again. If shortening is the culprit, she reasons, maybe no shortening at all would be even better.

That night, as she slides the biscuits off into the basket, each lands with an ominous thud. Her husband gamely takes a bite, or at least tries to. They might as well be hockey pucks.

I imagine that even non-cooks can see the point here. Each ingredient in the recipe makes a difference; each one is important and must not be left out—the shortening makes the biscuits tender, the flour gives them enough structure to hold together. Why are we smart enough to see that here, but forget it when it comes to spiritual matters?

One group says faith is the only thing we need. Another says strict obedience is the only thing we need. One of them bakes crumbs, the other hockey pucks.

Every generation reacts to the past generation's errors by

overcorrecting. Each group is so afraid of making the same mistake that they make another one, and worse, usually sneer at their fathers for missing it so badly, thinking in their youthful arrogance that they have discovered something brand new. What they have usually discovered is the same error another generation made long ago, the error their fathers tried to correct and overdid as well.

Why is it so hard to stop that swinging pendulum in the middle? Why do we arrogantly suppose that the last group did *everything* wrong and we are doing *everything* right.

Does God want faith? Yes, "the righteous shall live by his faith" (Hab 2.4).

Does God want obedience? Yes, "to obey is better than sacrifice" (1 Sam 15.22).

Does God want our hearts? He always has, and why can't we put it all together? "Thanks be to God...that you became *obedient from the heart*" (Rom 6.17).

The Hebrew write equates disobedience with a lack of faith. "And to whom did he swear that they should not enter into his rest but to them who were disobedient? And we see that they were not able to enter in due to unbelief" Heb 3.18–19).

Can God make it any plainer? He doesn't want crumbs; He doesn't want hockey pucks; He wants a nice tender biscuit of a heart that is firm enough to hold the shape of the pattern used to cut it. Follow the recipe God gave you. When you go about your day today, make sure you have all the ingredients.

Woe to you scribes, Pharisees, hypocrites! For you tithe mint, anise, and cumin, and have left undone the weightier matters of the law. But these [matters of the heart] *you ought to have done, and not left the other* [matters of strict obedience] *undone.*

Matthew 23.23

9. Chicken and Dumplings

I was reading a cooking magazine a few months ago which claimed to have formulated the best recipe for chicken and dumplings—one of my family's favorite meals, as well as a great way to stretch a dollar of the weekly grocery budget. Halfway through the article I found a big problem.

This magazine is based in Boston, its editor from Vermont. I already had a suspicion what their "best" recipe would contain—big puffy dumplings resembling drowned biscuits. In the South we prefer flat "slicker style" dumplings, akin to noodles or pasta, enriched with egg yolks and butter, even chicken fat if possible.

Sure enough, near the end of the article we readers were informed that the panel of tasters greatly preferred the "Yankee style" dumplings (their wording, not mine), "except for two holdouts from Kentucky." Really? Do you suppose if the magazine had been based in Atlanta, with the panel predominantly Southern, that the results might have been overwhelmingly in favor of the Southern style dumplings "except for two holdouts from Connecticut"?

Taste has a lot to do with your background, what you grew up eating, what your parents did and did not like, and what was available in your area. My boys loved fried okra. Some of the friends they brought home from college didn't even know what it was, and were almost afraid to try it. We are blessed to live in a society so wealthy that we can choose what we like and don't like. For most of us, eating has more to do with pleasure than necessity.

Unfortunately, that spoiled attitude has spilled over into our spiritual lives. We think we can take it or leave it as we choose, without ill effect; and if we take it, we think we can choose *how* we take it. Our Creator doesn't get to choose how He wants to be served. We get to choose how, when, where, even if. We get to choose which parts of this law we want to follow, and which we want to ignore. We can even interpret it any way we like, even if our interpretation ignores the context or plainly contradicts another part of it. We get to do all this choosing and He must be satisfied with what *we* want, and what *we* like. No wonder anthropologists talk about Deity as something each culture creates.

Yes, each culture creates gods they want to worship, but that is not Deity. Until we understand that the concept of Deity does not involve our likes and dislikes at all, we will never be approved by that Deity. As long as we think our opinions matter, we are not serving God, we are simply serving ourselves.

God is immutable. Truth is absolute. Obedience is not a request but a demand. We *can* choose to disobey, but the consequences will not be pleasant.

Thus says Jehovah, the King of Israel, and his Redeemer, Jehovah of hosts: I am the first, and I am the last; and besides me there is no God. And who, as I, shall call, and shall declare it, and set it in order for me, since I established the ancient people? And the things that are coming, and that shall come to pass, let them declare. Fear not, neither be afraid: have I not declared unto you of old, and showed it? And you are my witnesses. Is there a God besides me? Yea, there is no Rock; I know not any.

Isaiah 44.6–8

10. Boiling It Down

I have several recipes that call for making a reduction sauce as the last step. The pan in which the meat was cooked is filled with broth or some other thin liquid, the drippings in the pan deglazed, then the sauce boiled down to half or less the original volume, and herbs or perhaps a pat of butter whisked in at the end. Not only is the sauce thickened, but most important of all, the flavors are concentrated. I have heard trained chefs say that the reduction sauce can make or break the final product.

I love those passages in the Bible where the writer seems to boil down a complex situation into two or three simple things. Suddenly everything becomes clear. I know what is important because the complex flavors are concentrated enough for me to distinguish them.

Micah writes what has to be the best of these concentrated passages: "With what shall I come before Jehovah and bow myself before the high God? Shall I come before him with burnt offerings, with calves a year old? Will Jehovah be pleased with thousands of rams, with ten thousands of rivers of oil? Shall I give my firstborn for my transgression, the fruit of my body for the sin of my soul? He has shown you, o man, what is good, and *what does Jehovah require of you but to do justly, to love kindness, and to walk humbly with your God*" (6.6–8).

Far from releasing us from the minute details of God's law, it says this, "Be righteous, be kind to others, and be humble before God." What kind of man will argue with God about what

He requires, or even consider that any part of His law does not need obeying? Certainly not a humble one.

James boils it down 1.27: "Pure religion and undefiled before our God and Father is to visit the fatherless and the widows in their affliction and keep oneself unspotted from the world." As is the case in many of this type of passage, the widows and orphans are symbolic of anyone who needs help. In that day and time they were the helpless ones, the ones their society often ignored and oppressed, so it was natural to use them as a synecdoche. Be kind to others, James said, and later on in more detail (ch 2), help those who need your help, no matter what kind of help that might be, no matter how rich or poor, how important or unimportant by the world's standards. But don't forget to keep yourself pure, he adds, which can cover the gamut—anything from sexual immorality to sins of the heart to disobedience of any command of God. In seventeen words, he covers it all. Amazing.

Those verbal reductions are powerful. A list of commands or sins can often become ho-hum when we read them. Something in us instantly tries to categorize them and rank them. It becomes a matter of "what I can get away with" instead of what I need to do to be pleasing to God. But boil it down to a few words and suddenly it is all important. I need to focus on it all because it all hangs together or falls apart, something many of the Pharisees, and many of us, never seem to understand.

Those sauces poured over the dish right before serving have ceased to be individual ingredients. Instead they have become something else entirely, an amalgamation of ingredients blended so well they never separate. The goal for us is to become something new too, a person who no longer has to think about whether he will do right or wrong, but who automatically does it—a new creature who concentrates on goodness to man and humility before God, no longer questioning but instantly obeying from the heart.

Do you need a little more boiling?

And one of them, a lawyer, asked him a question to test him. Teacher, which is the great commandment in the law? [And so Jesus himself boiled it down to this] *You shall love the Lord your God with all your heart and with all your soul and with all your mind. This is the great and first commandment. And a second is like it, You shall love your neighbor as yourself.* **On these two commandments depend all the Law and the Prophets.**

Matthew 22.35–40

11. Picky Eaters

The other day I was talking with a friend who loves to cook as much as I do. We both spoke of how much more fun it is to cook for people who are not picky eaters. When all that effort sits in the bowls and platters on the table with scarcely a dent made in them because this one prefers this and that one prefers that, it is hard not to be offended. The very fact that I know so many more picky eaters these days than I did as a child emphasizes how wealthy this society has become. Hungry people are not picky eaters.

Real hunger is not a concept we understand. We eat by the clock instead of by our stomachs, which may be the biggest reason so many of us are overweight. If we only ate when we were truly hungry, would we eat too much on a regular basis? A celebratory feast, which used to happen only once or twice a year, has become a weekly, if not daily, occurrence for many.

And because we do not understand true physical hunger, we cannot understand Jesus' blessing upon those who hunger and thirst after righteousness. We think being willing to sit through one sermon a week makes us worthy, when that is probably the shallowest application of that beatitude. We don't want a spiritual feast. We want something light, with fewer calories, requiring little effort to eat. In fact, sometimes we want to be fed too. Spiritual eating has become too much trouble.

How many of us skip Bible classes? How many daydream during the sermons, plan the afternoon ahead, even text message each other? If more than one adult class is offered on Sunday mornings, how many choose the one that requires more study or deeper thinking? When extra classes are offered during the week, what percentage of the church actually chooses to attend? How many of us are actively pursuing our own studies at home, studies beyond that needed for the Sunday morning class? If we won't even eat the meals especially prepared for us by others, how in the world will we seek righteousness on our own and how will we ever progress past simple Bible study in satisfying our spiritual hunger?

Picky eaters suddenly become omnivores when they really need to eat. For some reason we think we can fast from spiritual food and still survive. Amazing how we can deceive ourselves so easily.

So, what's on your menu today, or have you even planned one?

Oh how love I your law! It is my meditation all the day. Your commandments make me wiser than my enemies; for they are ever with me. I have more understanding than all my teachers; for your testimonies are my meditation. I understand more than the aged, because I have kept your precepts. I have refrained my feet from every evil way, that I might observe your word. I have not turned aside from your ordinances; for You have taught me. How sweet are your words to my taste! sweeter than honey to my mouth! Through your precepts I get understanding: therefore I hate every false way.

Psalm 119.97–104

12. Product Shrinkage

I reached for a can of tuna the other day and absently read the label: Net Wt, 5 ounces. I can remember, and actually have recipes calling for a 7½ ounce can of tuna. I also remember 1 pound bags of coffee and 7 ounce bars of soap.

What happened? The manufacturers attempted to camouflage rising prices by putting less product in similar size containers for the same price. That morning I must have strained a full ounce of water from that 5 ounce can of tuna. I needed nearly two cans to make the same amount as 30 years ago. Eventually of course, the prices did rise. I can remember tuna for 29 cents a can. Either way, we get less for more.

That makes it even more amazing that the most expensive commodity on earth, the one that cost the death of the Son of God, is free. "To the praise of the glory of his grace, which he freely bestowed on us in the Beloved" (Eph 1.6).

I can recall hearing only one sermon on grace when I was a child. I guess that is why I remember it. I can even remember the building I was sitting in. We have too long ignored the fact that we are saved by grace because we are so afraid someone will think we believe in something unscriptural. Grace is one of the most scriptural topics there is!

But now that I hear more about the grace of God, I am noticing a different problem—we limit the grace of God to forgiveness.

Grace is there to help us live our lives as well. Paul says that when he prayed to Christ to rid him of his "thorn in the flesh,"

Christ's answer was, "My grace is sufficient." In other words, I will help you bear this burden.

Christ went on to say, "for my power is made perfect in weakness." As long as I try to handle things alone I will never make it. But when I make myself weak, allowing Christ to take care of me, I can handle anything. "Therefore," Paul adds, "I will boast all the more gladly of my weaknesses, so that the power of Christ may rest upon me" (2 Cor 12.9).

And there lies our problem: we so often will not let Him help us. We refuse, in the popular parlance, "to turn it over to God." We keep trying to help ourselves to the point that we do not even see the help He has offered. If it does not match our wants, if it does not look like the help we have envisioned, if it still involves bearing any burden at all, it can't be grace, and so we miss out, and have only ourselves to blame.

God says He will help. What else is it but grace that promises, "God is faithful, who will not suffer you to be tempted above that you are able; but will with the temptation make also the way of escape, that you may be able to endure it" (1 Cor 10.13)? If I do not endure, if I do not overcome, it is because I do not have faith in the grace of God. And that will have a huge impact because if I cannot trust it to help me through this life, how can I trust it to forgive me?

If we are willing to accept it, God will not hold back this gift. He will not decrease the amount of grace He gives. He will, in fact, increase it as we have need. *My grace is sufficient.*

Or maybe it's just that God's grace in any amount is far more powerful than any need we can ever imagine.

> *If the LORD had not been my help, my soul would soon have lived in the land of silence. When I thought, "My foot slips," your steadfast love, O LORD, held me up. When the cares of my heart are many, your consolations cheer my soul.*
>
> Psalm 94.17–19

13. Ultimate Ginger Cookies

Anyone who knows me knows that my favorite television cook is Ina Garten of "The Barefoot Contessa." I have saved very few recipes from the Food Channel, but of the few I have, the vast majority is hers.

One of my favorites is her "Ultimate Ginger Cookie." This is just about my favorite cookie *ever,* which is saying a lot for a cookie that doesn't have chocolate in it. It's a chewy cookie, something else I like, and I have added my own little twist by rolling the balls of dough in sparkling sugar before baking them. But what makes it "ultimate?" Not only does it have powdered ginger in it, but also over half a cup of chopped crystallized ginger. There is no question what kind of cookie this is—it's a *ginger* cookie.

I have several recipes with that word "ultimate" in the title. My "Ultimate Chocolate Chip Cookie" is good too. Not only does it have half again more chocolate chips than the usual recipe, but two kinds, bittersweet and milk chocolate. My "Ultimate Fudge Brownie" is maximum chocolate with minimal flour. My "Ultimate Peanut Butter Cookie" has no flour at all— just gobs of peanut butter, eggs, sugar and vanilla. Do you get the picture? "Ultimate" in a recipe means "a lot," "more than usual," and "well above average." "Ultimate" means there is no question what kind of cookie this is.

I started thinking about the word "Christian" in that context. Technically speaking, the word means "a disciple of Christ." That is not the way we use it today. "Christian" gets tacked on to anything that is even remotely religious. People can claim to be Christians just because they believe in a few of the Ten Commandments, which in itself is ironic when you understand the relationship of Christ to the Old Law. In our vernacular, Christians do not even have to be members of a church.

To keep that from rubbing off on us, maybe we should start thinking in terms of recipes. We should be "Ultimate Christians." If we are really followers of Christ we should be different from those who merely claim the name with a few allusions to prayer and God in their vocabulary.

Real disciples of Christ, by the definition of the word "disciple," are trying to be as much like their teacher as possible. They talk like he does and behave like he does. They know what commitment means—they serve as he did, sacrifice as he did, and fight the Devil like he did every day of his life. In fact, they are not afraid to acknowledge the devil as a real and dangerous being (like He did), even when others laugh at them for doing so. They condemn hypocrisy, especially among those who try to claim the same discipleship. They abhor sin, yet seek the vilest sinners in their own environment, knowing they are the ones who need their Master the most. They have compassion on the ill, the hated, and the lost. They will yield their lives to their Teacher by yielding their rights to others. They live by the Word of God, take comfort in the Spirit of God, and glory in their fellowship with them. In every decision, every event, and every aspect of their lives, they ask themselves how their Lord would have handled it. They are completely consumed with the spiritual; nothing else matters.

So, the question today is are we Christians in the modern vernacular, or are we real Christians, "Ultimate Christians?" Maybe if more of us started showing the world what the word "Christian" really means, we could stop making distinctions.

Whoever says he abides in him ought to walk in the same way in which he walked. ...A disciple is not above his teacher, but everyone when he is fully trained will be like his teacher.

1 John 2.6; Luke 6.40

14. Meat Loaf

There are probably as many recipes for meat loaf as there are families who eat it. Up until a few years ago, I thought the only excuse for making meat loaf was the sandwiches you made with the leftovers. In fact, I was happy to forego eating it at all the first night, and use it only for sandwiches the next day.

Then I found a recipe for Southwestern Meat Loaf. It's still meat loaf—ground meat, finely chopped vegetables, filler, binder of eggs and dairy, seasonings, and a tomato product on top.

Instead of white or yellow onions you use scallions. Instead of bell pepper, open a can of chopped green chiles. Instead of bread crumbs or oatmeal, grind up corn tortillas in the food processor. Instead of milk, sour cream fills the dairy bill with the usual eggs. Along with the usual salt and pepper, sprinkle in chili powder, cumin, and chopped fresh cilantro. Instead of ketchup, mix three tablespoons of brown sugar in a cup of salsa. Pour a quarter cup of that over the top; save the rest for heating and passing with the finished loaf. Fifteen minutes before it's done, sprinkle it with Monterey Jack cheese instead of cheddar. Voila! (Or whatever the Mexican word for that is.)

You know what? It still looks like meat loaf, smells like meat loaf, and tastes like meat loaf, just with a different accent, one we happen to prefer. But if someone else came up with a recipe using chunks of beef, broth, potatoes, onions, and carrots we would all think he was nuts to call it meat loaf. It bears no resemblance to the meat loaf pattern—it's beef stew.

For some reason, that made me think about God's plan for the church. We can find verse after verse where the apostles, particularly Paul, tell us that God expects us to follow a pattern in each congregation—1 Corinthians 4.17; 7.17; 16.1 and 2 Timothy 1.13, just to name a few. But sometimes we mistake an expedient for a flaw in the pattern, and try to legislate where God did not.

Take the Lord's Supper for instance: grape juice and unleavened bread on the first day of the week. What kind of grapes must the juice come from? What sort of flour must the bread be made of? Most of the time here in America, we use juice made from Concord grapes. They did not have Concord grapes in first century Jerusalem. The grapes they had in Corinth were probably different, too. Today we use wheat flour, usually bleached, all-purpose, white flour. Most likely the early Christians in Palestine used barley flour, and I bet there was nothing white about it—pure, whole grain was all most of them could afford. (Funny how that is the expensive kind today!) In Rome the Christians might have used semolina flour. But there is one thing for certain—everywhere in the world, grapes of some sort are available, and everywhere in the world people eat bread. All they have to do is press the grapes and remove the leavening from the bread recipe.

Following a pattern does not mean we make rules God did not. Two women can each make a dress from the same pattern. One uses satin and trims it in lace; the other can only afford gingham and trims it with rickrack. Did they both follow the pattern? Are the sleeves the same length in the same place? Is the neckline the same? Do they both have a gathered skirt, or is one A-line? Oops. That one changed the pattern. It's really not that hard to tell, is it?

And that is how we tell if a church is following the pattern. Sometimes we try to force every church into satin and lace, when they are really more suited to gingham and rickrack. But the essentials are there. It is not my job to go around making judgments about details (cultural expedients) as long as the basic pattern is sound.

But that pattern does matter. It has always mattered with God. Read about Nadab and Abihu, Uzzah, or King Uzziah. Then let's make sure we have found a group of people who do their best to follow God's pattern, and who do not add their own rules to God's. After all, meat loaf is meat loaf is meat loaf. But beef stew isn't!

> *Even as Moses is **warned of God** when he is about to make the tabernacle, See, said he, that you make all things according to the pattern which was shown you in the mount.*
>
> Hebrews 8.5

15. Eggshells

Some have called eggs the perfect food with their own perfect container. I recently heard a TV cook say they are "hermetically sealed." Eggshells themselves are stronger than their reputation says. After all, birds sit on them for days, and it takes a good deal of effort for a baby bird to peck its way out of one.

However, it doesn't take more than one instance of carelessness to discover just how easily they will break. Mine usually make it home from the grocery store in one piece, in spite of being placed in a cooler with a couple of bags of groceries and an ice block, and then traveling thirty miles, the last half mile over a bumpy lime rock lane. Only once in nearly 30 years have I opened my cooler to find eggs that have tumbled out and cracked all over the other groceries.

You must also be careful where you put them on the counter. Most recipes require ingredients at room temperature, so I take the butter and eggs out a half hour or more before I plan to use them. I quickly learned to put them in a small bowl so they couldn't possibly roll off the countertop onto the floor, even if I did think I had them safely corralled by other ingredients. Somehow they only roll when you turn your back. As I recall, that recipe required a lot of eggs, and suddenly I was short a couple.

Because of their relative fragility, we have developed the idiom "walking on eggshells." When the situation is tricky, when someone is already on a short fuse, we tread carefully with our words, as if we were walking carefully, trying not to break the eggshells under our feet. Sometimes that is a good thing. No one wants to hurt a person who has just experienced a tragedy. No one wants to carelessly bring up a topic that might hinder the growth of a babe in Christ. Certainly no one wants to put out a spark of interest in the gospel.

But sometimes the need to walk on eggshells is a shame, especially when the wrong people have to walk on them.

I suppose every congregation has one of those members who gives everyone pause; one who has hot buttons you do your best not to push; one who seems to take offense at the most innocuous statements or actions. The shame of it is this: in nearly every case I can remember, that person is over 50, and most over 60. "You know old brother so-and-so," everyone will tell newcomers. "You have to be careful what you say around him." Why is it that younger Christians must negotiate minefields around an older Christian who should have grown in wisdom and forbearance?

Do you think God has nothing to say about people like this?

> The vexation of a fool is known at once, but the prudent ignores an insult. (Prov 12.16)

> Hatred stirs up strife, but love covers all offenses. (Prov 10.12)

> Good sense makes one slow to anger, and it is his glory to overlook an offense. (Prov 19.11)

> Love bears all things, believes all things, hopes all things, endures all things. (1 Cor 13.7)

> Above all, keep loving one another earnestly, since love covers a multitude of sins. (1 Pet 4.8)

Now let's put that all together. A person who is quick to take offense, who is easily set off when a certain topic arises, who seems to make a career out of hurt feelings is a fool, imprudent, full of hate instead of love, divisive, and lacking good sense. That's what God says about the matter. He didn't walk on eggshells.

On the other hand, the person who overlooks insults, who

doesn't take everything the worst possible way, who makes allowances for others' foibles, especially verbal ones, and who doesn't tell everyone how hurt or insulted he is, is wise, prudent, sensible, and full of love. Shouldn't that describe any older Christian, especially one who has been at if for thirty or forty years?

So, let's take a good look at ourselves. Do people avoid me? Am I defensive, and quick to assume bad motives? Do I find myself insulted or hurt several times a week? Do I keep thinking that everyone is out to get me in every arena of life? Maybe I need to realize that I am not the one that everyone always has in mind when they speak or act. I am not, after all, the center of the universe. Maybe it's time I acted the spiritual age I claim to be.

Maybe I need to sweep up a few eggshells.

Put on then, as God's chosen ones, holy and beloved, compassionate hearts, kindness, humility, meekness, and patience, bearing with one another and, if one has a complaint against another, forgiving each other; as the Lord has forgiven you, so you also must forgive. And above all these put on love, which binds everything together in perfect harmony.

Colossians 3.12–14

16. Lessons from the Food Channel

I watch more Food Network shows than any others. I have one favorite I try to never miss, and a couple of others that I will watch if I have the time. Even reruns are good on the Food Channel.

Funny thing, though, I have only tried about half a dozen recipes from any of the shows I have watched. That's not per show; that's half a dozen total. The thing I get most from these shows is technique—learning that it takes more salt in your pasta water than you might think to really season it; that you should season every layer of a dish not just the final product so that the dish tastes seasoned not just salty; that meat continues to cook after you take it out of the oven so you must take it out before it's totally done or you end up with tough, dry meat; that in 90% of cases fresh herbs are far better than dried; and that real parmagiana reggiano is worth the money—not only does it taste that much better, but you actually use less for the same effect.. I didn't realize I was picking these things up until last Thanksgiving when I was told by three separate family members that it was the best turkey and dressing I had ever made.

I started thinking about that, and realized that is the way Satan gets to most of us, too. We don't go out and do all the big, bad sins in the world, following his personal recipes for evil. But if we are not careful, the worldly techniques find their way into our lives. Our perspectives change from the spiritual to the physical. We become more concerned about physical security than spiritual security, more prone to rely on our own acumen than God's promises, more willing to accept sin in others in order to get along.

I can remember preachers making jokes about the King James wording of 1 Peter 2.9: "Ye are...a peculiar people." We think peer pressure is only a problem for teenagers, but none of us wants to be called "peculiar." Four hundred years ago, when the KJV was translated, that word meant "private property." You see, we are supposed to be God's private property, not Satan's. We should be learning God's techniques, not the Devil's. And I guess in the way the word is used today, that *would* make us appear a little peculiar.

In just two or three hours a week, the Food Channel has changed my cooking. Just think what might be happening to us in the many hours a week we are surrounded by unspiritual people concerned about unspiritual things. Being aware will help us to keep the influence of their techniques minimal. Better still, we should surround ourselves every chance we get with those who would help us learn better spiritual techniques. Let's all help one another get to Heaven.

But you are an elect race, a royal priesthood, a holy nation, a people for God's own possession [peculiar], *that you may show forth the excellencies of him who called you out of darkness into his marvelous light; who in time past were no people, but now are the people of God; who had not obtained mercy, but now have obtained mercy.*

1 Peter 2.9–10

17. Just Dessert

Unfortunately, I have a sweet tooth. I have never understood rail thin women who complain about a dessert being "too sweet," "too rich," and certainly not, "too big." That probably explains why I am not rail thin.

I had a good excuse for making desserts with two active boys in the house. Their favorites were plain, as desserts go—blueberry pie, apple pie, Mississippi mud cake, and any kind of cheesecake. Nowadays, since there are only two of us and we two do not need a whole lot of sweets, desserts are usually for special occasions, and so they have gotten a little more "special" too. Coconut cake with lime curd filling and coconut cream cheese frosting; chocolate fudge torte with chocolate ganache filling, dark chocolate frosting, and peanut butter ganache trim, garnished with dry roasted peanuts; lemon sour cream cake with lemon filling and lemon cream cheese frosting; and a peanut butter cup cheesecake piled with chopped peanut butter cups and drizzled with hot fudge sauce; all these have found their way into my repertoire and my heart.

But one thing I have never done is feed my family on dessert alone. Dessert is for later, after you eat your vegetables, after the whole grain, high fiber, high protein meals, after you've taken your vitamins and minerals. Everyone knows that, except perhaps children, and I would have been a bad mother had I given in to their desires instead of doing what was best for them.

So why do we expect God to feed us nothing but dessert? Why do we think life must always be easy, fun, and exciting?

Why is it that the only time I say, "God is good," is when I get what I want?

God is good even when He makes me eat my vegetables, when I have to choke down the liver, and guzzle the V8. God is good when I undergo trials and misfortunes. God is good even when the devil tempts me sorely. He knows what is best for me, what will make me strong and able to endure, and, ultimately, He knows that living a physical life on this physical earth forever is not in my best interests.

Eating nothing but cake and pie and pastries will create a paradox—an obese person who is starving to death, unable to grow and become strong. God knows what we need and gives it to us freely and on a daily basis. He doesn't fill us up with empty spiritual calories. He doesn't give us just dessert. Truly, God is good.

Rejoice the soul of your servant, for unto you O LORD, do I lift up my soul. For you Lord are good, and ready to forgive and abundant in lovingkindness unto all them who call upon you. …There is none like you among the gods, O LORD, neither any works like your works. All nations whom you have made shall come and worship before you, O LORD, and they shall glorify your name. For you are great and do wondrous things. You are God alone.

Psalm 86.4–5, 8–10

18. Pitting Cherries

I just pitted two pounds of fresh cherries. I *knew* there was a reason I liked blueberries better.

Even with a handy-dandy little cherry pitter, it is still quite a chore. You have to do them one at a time, well over a hundred, and sometimes the pit does not come out the first try. You have to fiddle with the cherry until you get it in there just right—so the little plunger will go right through the center. Then there is the clean-up as some of those wayward pits bounce across the counter and floor, staining everything cherry red.

Not worth it you say? You have obviously never had a cherry pie made with anything but canned cherry pie filling! Some things are worth the trouble. Like children. Like marriage. Like living according to God's rules.

Satan will do everything in his power to make it seem otherwise. He will tell you his reward here and now is greater, like a ready-made store-bought pie. He will tell you that God's reward is mediocre, like a pie you can have in the oven in ten minutes with canned filling and refrigerated pie crust. He will tell you God's reward does not even exist, that there is no such thing as a pie with a homemade crust and fresh cherries—it's all an illusion. Everyone knows pies come in a box in the freezer case!

But God's reward is real; it is better than anything this life and that Enemy have to offer. It takes some effort. Sometimes we fail and have to try again. Sometimes people make fun of us. Sometimes we work till our backs ache and our fingers cramp up, but when you put God's reward on the window sill to cool, everyone knows it was worth it. Even the ones who won't get to taste it.

> *Blessed are you when men shall hate you, and when they shall separate you from their company, and reproach you, and cast out your name as evil, for the Son of man's sake. Rejoice in that day, and leap for joy, for behold, great is your reward in Heaven. ... So that men shall say, "Truly there is a reward for the righteous; truly there is a God who judges the earth."*
>
> Luke 6.22–23; Psalm 58.11

19. Countertops

It is axiomatic: men cannot see dirt.

Whenever Keith leaves the kitchen, I enter it, looking for the mess he has left. No, it is not obvious, especially when you have a mottled medium shade of brown countertop. But as a woman, I automatically know to wipe a countertop after I have done anything on top of it. He thinks because he cannot see it, it isn't there. So I wipe up cracker crumbs, cookie crumbs, salt, coffee grounds, peanut butter smears, and assorted beverage circles several times a day.

That doesn't mean he is dirty. If I ask him to clean the tub for me, you will have never heard such scrubbing and scouring and huffing and puffing in all your life. It sparkles when he is finished. Whenever he washes dishes for me, he will spend a good half hour on a black pot bottom I have long since given up on. No, he is not dirty. He is just not used to looking for the mess until I ask him to. Then he makes the effort with an eye to what is not clean, and suddenly, he sees it.

We all have that problem when looking for the dirt in our own lives. We simply cannot see it. But in someone else? That's simple, and it is so because we have an eye for the dirt in others' lives, especially those we don't like much.

Many country wives tell their husbands again and again that it is impossible to get all the dirt and mud off those athletic shoes and work boots with the deep treads on the bottom. "But I wiped my feet," they say, and walk right in, shoes and all.

Then after they leave, we women get out the brooms and the dustpans, or in some cases, the mops and pails.

Some people just will not believe you when you tell them over and over and over that their actions will cost them their souls, that they will become inured to worldliness and think nothing of it, and that other people will suffer because of the dirt they leave behind them. They reach the point that they blind themselves to the obvious facts in front of them.

Today, make it a point to look for the dirt in your own life instead of others'. Do it while you still *can* see it. One of these days even a microscope won't help, and then where will you be? You will find yourself living a life full of dirt and stains that would have disgusted you not long before, but which has become invisible to you. You will find yourself eating off a filthy countertop of sin that will kill you with its toxic germs sooner or later.

And why behold the mote that is in your brother's eye, but consider not the beam that is in your own eye? How will you say to your brother, Let me pull the mote out of your eye; and, behold, a beam is in your own eye? You hypocrite, first cast the beam out of your own eye; and then shall you see clearly to cast the mote out of your brother's eye.

Matthew 7.3–5

20. Blueberry Crisp

I have gotten lazy. When I need a quick dessert, I pull a quart of blueberries out of the freezer, cut together a cup of flour, a cup of sugar, and a stick of butter, spread those crumbs on top of the blueberries in a baking dish and bake it for about 45 minutes. Suddenly I have a warm, bubbly, fruity filling with a sweet crunchy topping for a minimum of work and mess in the kitchen. While a pastry chef would not be impressed, for most people it's just fine.

But a blueberry pie? Now that takes a commitment. First you make the crust, a careful process of measuring, handling, rolling and fitting into the pie plate. Then you make the filling, far more ingredients than a crisp and more careful measuring. Then you have to deal with the top crust, rolling it, sealing it, crimping it, and preparing it for baking with a vent, a brush of milk and a sprinkling of sparkling sugar. And the baking? First ten minutes at 425, then another 35–45 at 350, carefully watching the top for over-browning and the vent for bubbling blueberries. If they don't bubble, it isn't done yet no matter how brown the crust is. So then you must lay some foil over the top so it won't burn before it finishes baking. It's a real process.

Then you look around the kitchen at the two mixing bowls, the many measuring cups and spoons, the wooden spoons, pastry cutter, and spatulas, the flour covered countertop, and often the floor as well. It takes more than a minute to clean it up. But which has the best combination of flavors and textures? Which one is more likely to get the oohs and aahs of company? When

I really want to do something nice for someone, and assuming time is not an issue, they get the pie.

Too many of us make God settle for the crisp. If it's easy and convenient, God gets the service. If I can still have my life the way I want it, with my own priorities in order, then fine—I am happy to be a Christian. If it appeals to my sense of sweetness and light, and pats on the back rather than rebukes and chastening, if I receive tons of blessings and few if any trials, I am happy to do it. Becoming a child of God means repentance, and repentance means I am sorry, right? So I say I am and now I can go back to doing whatever I want to do. Don't expect any tears or humility.

God will not accept me on those terms. Nearly every gospel sermon you can find in the New Testament mentions repentance, but simply being sorry is not the repentance those preachers are talking about. Second Kings 22.19 says Josiah's heart was tender and he humbled himself. David says he acknowledged his sin and did not hide from God (Psa 32.5) and that God only accepts "a broken spirit and a broken and contrite heart" (Psa 51.17). John told the crowds to "bring forth fruits worthy of repentance" (Matt 3.8), and Jeremiah reminded Old Testament Israel to "*thoroughly* amend" their ways (Jer 7.5).

Repentance is not cosmetic. It is a complete change of heart and life, and a wholesale attitude adjustment when considering your lifestyle, its goals and purposes. Paul commends the Corinthians for a repentance that "wrought care, indignation, fear, longing, zeal, avenging" (2 Cor 7.11). Commitment to God cannot come without that kind of repentance.

Repentance is the very key to conversion. Once you repent in the way those Corinthians did, in the way the early Christians did, no one will be able to keep you from doing the rest because now everything has changed. You will not argue about whether baptism is essential. You will not argue about how many times you need to assemble with the saints. You will not argue about whether something is "right" or "wrong" if there is any question at all, because you will have the zeal, the care, and the longing to do everything you possibly can to serve God.

What did you make for God when you became a Christian? If you only gave him a blueberry crisp, it's time to get out the mixing bowls and try again.

> *If my people, who are called by my name, shall humble themselves, and pray, and seek my face, and turn from their wicked ways; then will I hear from heaven, and will forgive their sin, and will heal their land.*
>
> 2 Chronicles 7.14

21. The Acid Test

It is a culinary fact that fat tempers acid. That is why some of the world's favorite dishes combine a good helping of both. Melted mozzarella offsets a tomato-y pizza sauce. A cheese-stuffed calzone is almost unbearably rich without a small bowl of marinara to dip it in. A homemade pimento cheese sandwich *screams* for a homemade dill pickle on the side. The South's favorite summer treat, a drippy tomato sandwich on high quality white bread, simply *must* be slathered with a glop of mayo. Fat and acid—the perfect combination; it's why we dip French fries in ketchup and chips in salsa; it's why the favorite toppings for a hot dog are ketchup, mustard, relish, and chili. It's why we put whipped cream on strawberries and why a Key lime pie is just about the perfect dessert.

Trials, tribulations, sufferings and afflictions are the acid tests for Christians. No one wants to go through them, yet we all understand that is what makes us stronger, builds up our faith, keeps us able to endure till the end. All of us would be spiritual wimps without them.

What we fail to realize is that God gives us plenty of fat to offset them. How many blessings can you count in your life today, not even considering the most wonderful one of all, your salvation? How many good things happened to you *just this morning?* Did your car start? Did you make it to work safely? Are your children safely ensconced in a safe place? Do you still have a roof over your head? Is there food in your refrigerator? Is the electricity on, the water running and the AC humming away? Are their flowers blooming in your yard and birds singing in the trees? Do you have pleasant memories to calm you in the midst of sorrows? Is there a Bible in your home and are you free to read it whenever you want to? Did you pray to a Father who loves you more than anything else? How many more "fat" items can we come up with? Probably enough to fill even the gigabytes of memory in our computers if we just took the time to think of them. If you have trouble, just ask a three-year-old—they are pros at this.

I don't mean to make light of people's problems with this little analogy—but then again, maybe I do. Paul calls them "light afflictions" in 2 Corinthians 4, and he was including persecution to the death in that context. Compared to the end result, compared to the reward, compared to our Savior's sufferings so we could have that reward, our trials and tribulations are light indeed.

So today, if you are in the middle of a struggle, if the acid is burning your soul, look for the fat God gave you to temper it. Look for everything good in your day, in your life, no matter how small it may seem. If that doesn't work, and sometimes it doesn't, remember the good that will result from your testing, and don't let it be for nothing. Don't let Satan win. The bigger the tomato, the more mayo God smears on, *if you only know where to look.*

> *Wherefore we faint not, for though our outer man is decaying, our inward man is renewed day by day. For this momentary light affliction works for us more and more exceedingly an eternal weight of glory;* **while we look not at things which are seen, but at the things which are not seen; for the things which are seen are temporal, but the things which are not seen are eternal.**

> 2 Corinthians 4.16–18

22. The Refrigerator Door

Some things are just not supposed to happen. Sooner or later you will have a flat tire. Sooner or later your AC will quit on you. Sooner or later the washer will stop washing and the dryer will stop drying. None of these things are pleasant, but they all happen to everyone. When it happens, you groan and then get on with the business of life. But some things are just not supposed to happen.

I was putting some things in the refrigerator the other day. Usually the door swings shut by itself, but this time, as I twisted to get the next item, it swung all the way open. Then it quietly fell off its hinges and tumbled shelf side down, dumping pickles, olives, ketchup, three kinds of mustard, Worcestershire and soy sauces, homemade jelly, butter, cream cheese, and my super special ordered-from-California eye medicine onto the floor, leaving the rest of the refrigerator wide open and humming. For a moment I just stood there, stunned. We have been through several refrigerators—a couple of cheap ones that came with the apartment or trailer we were renting at the time, and a couple of secondhand ones. But this one was a recommended model we bought new. Never have we had a refrigerator door fall off, not even the inexpensive or used ones. Refrigerator doors *do not* fall off.

Don't you know that is how God feels at times? We can find several passages where he laments our actions, saying, "This is not supposed to happen," at least in substance, if not verbatim. James 3.10 is a prime example: "Out of the same mouth comes forth blessing and cursing. My brothers, these things ought not so to be." James tells us we should not bless God and then curse man because when we curse a man made in the image of God, we might as well be cursing God. Yikes! That puts another spin on it, doesn't it? Understand, we are not talking about using four letter words here, but about maliciously wishing evil upon a person. We are not supposed to do it—not even to other drivers! And James acts like we ought to know this *without being told: we should not be cursing men!*

Unfortunately, we do not know, or willfully ignore, many such things. We should know God is our Creator and worship him, but for some reason that is hotly debated even among intelligent people. We should know God's law; he has made it available and easy enough to understand. But even in the church we have "seasoned" Christians who cannot find their way from Acts to Habakkuk without getting lost somewhere in Ephesians, and who think John wrote several "Revelations."

I wonder if God does what I did the other morning, stand there in shock, staring at a door-less refrigerator, with my mouth hanging open, thinking, "What? That just doesn't happen." Unfortunately, it does. You wonder if God is really all that surprised any more. Tell you what, let's work on a real surprise for him—let's make sure *we* don't do any of those things from now on.

> *The ox knows his owner, and the ass his master's crib; but Israel does not know, my people do not consider. ...Yes, the stork in the heavens knows her appointed times; and the turtledove and the swallow and the crane observe the time of their coming; but my people know not the law of Jehovah.*
>
> Isaiah 1.3; Jeremiah 8.7

23. Stinkbugs

While I have kept three or four potted herbs on my steps for several years, it has only been a short while that I have grown an herb garden—two kinds of parsley, three kinds of basil, plus thyme, oregano, marjoram, dill, sage, cilantro, rosemary, mint, and chives.

I'm still learning some things the hard way. Dill must be planted in late fall because it cannot tolerate the heat of a Florida summer. Basil will stop growing when the weather cools, whether you protect it from the frost or not. Oregano is a ground runner and needs a lot of room. You must snip your chives from the bottom—not just trim off the tops—if you expect them to replenish. One recipe for pesto will decimate a basil plant for at least two weeks. Always give mint its own separate bed, or better still, pot, because it will take over the joint if you don't.

And, Keith hates cilantro. Although I am not exactly sure how he knows this, he says it tastes "like stinkbugs." We discovered this when I sprinkled chopped fresh cilantro over a turkey tortilla casserole. Now cilantro does have a distinctive flavor. While it bears a close physical resemblance to Italian flat-leaf parsley, the strongest flavored parsley, its flavor is probably ten times stronger than that herb. There *is* such a thing as too much cilantro. On the other hand, a lot of people like it in moderation, including me. I guess there is no accounting for tastes.

And that is why some people reject Jesus. To some people life tastes sweeter when we do things His way. The difficult times become easier to bear, and the good times more than we dared hope for. But other people see in Him a restrictive cage denying them all the pleasures of life. Their focus on the here and now keeps them from seeing the victory of Eternity, but even worse, they are blinded by Satan to the true joys a child of God can have in this life as well. "And exercise yourself unto godliness; for bodily exercise is profitable for a little, but godliness is profitable for all things, *having the promise of the life that now is,* and of that which is to come" (1 Tim 4.7–8). We can have joy, peace, hope, love, and fellowship with both God and the best people on earth, *while* on this earth.

But they just can't see it. I guess to them, godliness tastes like stinkbugs. Truly, there is just no accounting for tastes.

> *For we are a sweet smell of Christ unto God, in them that are saved, and in them that perish; to the one a smell from death unto death, and to the other a smell from life unto life.*
>
> 2 Corinthians 2.15–16

24. Pie Crust

I grew up watching my mother make her own pie crust. It never crossed my mind that was unusual, that there were convenience products, including ready-made pie crusts, at the grocery store. So I was thoroughly spoiled as a child. Homemade pie crust was all I ever had.

Unfortunately, I married and moved a thousand miles away without getting that recipe and the special instructions that probably went along with it. I lived closer to my in-laws then and, as luck would have it, they had owned a small town bakery, so I asked them for their recipe. What I got was a ratio; otherwise I would have wound up with a recipe beginning, "fifty pounds of flour...." It went like this: half as much shortening as flour, half as much water as shortening.

It took a few years, but I finally got the hang of it. I also discovered the proper ratio of salt (a scant teaspoon per two cups of flour), the advantage of ice water rather than plain tap water (it makes the crust flakier), and the need to handle the dough as little as possible if you want to be able to eat it instead of use it as a Frisbee.

I still have a little difficulty passing this recipe along. You see, flour changes according to the humidity. If it has soaked up moisture from the air, it will take less water. How do you tell? By the way it feels. How does it feel? Here the problem lies. When everything is right, it feels right, that's how you tell. But how does "right" feel? It feels like pie crust dough that is "right." There is no way to describe it if you haven't ever put your hands in it before.

The same thing happens when I am trying to help a person with just about any recipe—biscuits, cookie dough, cake batter, gravy, cream sauce—when it's right, you know it. In fact, when teaching someone to make gravy or béchamel, I have to take the spoon from them into my hand and give it a stir so I can feel it in order to *really* know. That's why I never make my pastry crust in a food processor—I can't feel it!

The trick is to do it over and over and over for *years*. That's how you know what "right" is. Yes, you must have a good recipe, but even a good recipe can turn out wrong if you are not familiar with it.

Do you want to know how to avoid false doctrine? It has nothing to do with studying every possible false teaching out there. You would have no time for it. What you do is study the real thing over and over and over for *years*. Then when the false one comes along it won't feel quite the same, and you will suddenly catch yourself saying, "Unh, unh. Something's not right here." Because you are so familiar with what "right" is, you will have far less trouble seeing what "wrong" is.

Learning the facts may seem formalistic. It may seem like our religion is lacking some "heart." Don't be so quick to judge. Some of the people most likely to be taken captive by false prophets are those who love the whir and excitement of "food processor" religion. "Wow! Look at it go. Look how fast it comes together. This must surely be the real thing." It is certainly more rousing than watching someone cut a cup of shortening into two cups of flour with a handheld pastry blender, up and down, over and over, for several tedious minutes. But that food processor religion is more likely to be tough and overworked or wet and hard to handle, while the handmade religion will separate into flaky layers of depth, and rival the filling itself for the starring role.

There is no short cut for this kind of experience. If it takes years of handling pastry crust to reach this level of comfortable, secure familiarity, God's word certainly won't be any easier, but what should we expect? God didn't write pulp fiction.

> *And this I pray that your love may abound yet more and more in knowledge and all discernment; so that you may distinguish the things that differ; that you may be sincere and void of offence unto the day of Christ; being filled with the fruits of righteousness, which are through Jesus Christ, unto the glory and praise of God.*
>
> Philippians 1.9–11

25. Mason Jars

Do people even know what Mason jars are any more? My favorite store has stopped carrying them, and when I finally found them at the local discount store, I could have bought out their entire stock without overdrawing my bank account.

I have a large supply of those clear sturdy jars. Every year I stuff them with pickles, jams, tomatoes, and salsa, place them in a canner and subject them to more heat and pressure than a football coach in the midst of a losing season. Every year they seal and protect as they sit on my shelves for the next few months, then are emptied, washed, and placed back in the shed until I need them again.

This year three or four of them broke. I lifted the lid off the canner, and as I peered into the steam, there they sat, emptied of liquid but looking intact until I tried to lift them out and the bottom stayed in the water, while the sides and lid hung from the canning ring. The contents, now limp and useless, toppled into the canning water. I could hardly complain. These jars have served me well for years. Now that we are only two and I don't need as much, I have plenty of others to take their places on the shelves.

Those broken jars have made canning especially exciting this past year. I never know what I will find when I lift the lids off my two canners. They have also made me think about the way God uses the image of jars in the Bible. As with many other things, He presents them in two ways, one I want and the other I don't.

He tells Isaiah, "Wherefore thus says the Holy One of Israel, Because you despise this word, and trust in oppression and perverseness, and rely thereon; therefore this iniquity shall be to you as a breach ready to fall, swelling out in a high wall, whose breaking comes suddenly in an instant. And he shall break it as a potter's vessel is broken, breaking it in pieces without sparing; so that there shall not be found among the pieces thereof a shard wherewith to take fire from the hearth, or to dip up water out of the cistern (30.12–14). God's promise of destruction for his rebellious people is frightening, and we must be careful for it does not need to be a national destruction. He can do the same thing to rebellious individuals.

But God also holds out a reward for faithful service that is almost too amazing to believe. "And he who overcomes, and he who keeps my works unto the end, to him will I give authority over the nations: and he shall rule them with a rod of iron, as the vessels of the potter are broken to shivers; as I also have received of my Father: and I will give him the morning star. He who has ears, let him hear what the Spirit says to the churches" (Rev 2.26–29).

I do believe in that reward, and so should you. God has shown us that He will fulfill His promises. That promise in Isaiah is historically verifiable down to the last detail. This one would be too, if history were to continue after it occurs. It won't, but we will.

Now in a great house there are not only vessels of gold and of silver, but also of wood and of earth; and some unto honor, and some unto dishonor. If a man therefore purge himself from these, he shall be a vessel unto honor, sanctified, meet for the master's use, prepared unto every good work.

2 Timothy 2.20–21

26. Fried Okra

If you are from north of the Mason-Dixon line, please don't turn the page! I have converted not only several children, but several Northerners to this Southern delicacy. It's all about taking the problems and turning them to your advantage—and being patient.

The problem with okra, if you'll pardon the expression, is the slime. One reason it was used in gumbos was its thickening power, which is a nicer way of referring to that viscous property. My family just calls it what it is. It doesn't bother them because they know what I can do with that--stuff.

Follow these directions closely. Use a colander, not a bowl, when you slice it. You will still get the goo on your knife and a little on your hands—my method won't fix that—but it will disappear when you cook it.

Slice it about a half inch thick, discarding the stem end and the tails. If it has been in the fridge a few days, it might need a little coaxing to release some of its "juices." If so, put that colander in the sink and scatter a few drops of water here and there from a wet hand. Don't deluge it. If it's already good and gooey, don't bother. Sprinkle it with salt, then with flour, *not corn meal*. (My mother taught me that and we are both GRITS—Girls Raised in the South.) Stir it to coat. Now walk away. In five minutes come back. If it's dry, do the water trick again, just a sprinkle. Add more salt and more flour and stir it again. Walk away again. You may need to do this several times, allowing the excess flour to fall through the holes in the colander into the sink where you can wash it away—loose flour will burn in the bottom of a skillet.

After about fifteen minutes and maybe as many as five applications of flour and salt, the flour will have adhered to the "slime" and, magically, the okra will have made its own batter. It will stick together in clumps like caramel corn, which is exactly what you want.

Heat a half inch of vegetable oil in a skillet. Put in one piece of okra and wait till it starts bubbling and sizzling. Slowly add only as much okra as there is room in the pan. Since it tends to stick together, you will need to mash it out to spread it around. Now walk away and leave it again. No fiddling with it, no turning it, no stirring it.

In about ten minutes you will begin to see browning around the edges. When that happens you can start turning it. The second side will brown faster, as will the entire second batch. Watch your oil; you may need to turn it down if the browning begins to happen *too* quickly. Drain it on paper towels.

You will now have the crunchiest okra you ever ate. No slime, no weird flavor, nothing but crunch. You cannot eat this with a fork—it rolls off, or if you try to stab it, it shatters. This is Southern finger food, a delicacy we eat at least twice every summer before we start pickling it or giving it away. Too much fried food is not healthy they tell us, but everyone needs a lube job once in awhile.

The trick to that okra is patiently using the problem itself to overcome it—given enough time, that slime makes a batter that is better than anything you could whip up on your own with half a dozen ingredients.

Patience is a virtue for Christians too, not just cooks. How do you make it through suffering? You patiently endure it (2 Cor 1.6), and you remember its purpose and use it for that purpose. Patiently enduring suffering will make you a joint-heir with Christ (Rom 8.17–18). It will make you worthy of the kingdom (2 Thes 1.4–5). If we suffer with him, we will reign with him (2 Tim 2.12). Only those who share in his suffering will share in his comfort (2 Cor 1.7).

But none if this works if you don't patiently endure the suffering. If you give up, you lose. If you turn against God, he will turn against you. If you refuse the fellowship of Christ's suffering, he will refuse you. We must use that suffering to make ourselves stronger and worthy to be his disciple. Just like I am happy to have a particularly "slimy" bowl of okra to worth with, knowing it will produce the crunch I want, the early Christians "rejoiced that they were counted worthy to suffer" (Acts 5.41). They knew it would make them better disciples of their Lord. We can understand these things when it comes to something as mundane as fried okra. Why can't we recognize it in far more important matters? We even have a trite axiom about this—when life gives you lemons, make lemonade. When life gives you trials, make yourself a stronger person.

After suffering, Peter promises that God will restore, confirm, strengthen and establish us (1 Pet 5.10). He is talking to those who endure, who use the suffering to their advantage and become better people. Remind yourself of the promises God gives to those who suffer. Remind yourself of the rewards. Remind yourself every day that it's worth it. The New Testament writers did, so it is no shame if you do it too.

> *The Spirit himself bears witness with our spirit that we are children of God, and if children, then heirs—heirs of God and fellow heirs with Christ, provided we suffer with him in order that we may also be glorified with him. For I consider that the sufferings of this present time are not worth comparing with the glory that is to be revealed to us.*
>
> Romans 8.16–18

27. Sage Advice

I get these questions so often, let's kill two birds with one stone today.

Q. How do you use all those herbs you grow?
A. Dill is good in any mayonnaise based salad—potato salad, tuna salad, macaroni salad, etc. I also use it in my own homemade tartar sauce and deviled eggs.

Basil is good in anything with tomatoes. Throw the leaves of red basil leaves whole in a salad for color as well as taste. When using basil in long cooking items like marinara, be sure to add another sprinkle fresh at the end, just before serving. And anyone with a basil plant needs to learn how to make pesto, the ultimate basil sauce.

Rosemary goes with poultry, pork, and lamb. Sage goes with poultry, pork and beef. Thyme is good with chicken and beef. Tarragon is good with veal and chicken, particularly chicken salad. Use chives when you want a mild onion flavor but not the sharpness of a raw onion. Parsley goes just about anywhere, and not just for garnish.

At Thanksgiving, think of Simon and Garfunkel when you season your bird: "parsley, sage, rosemary, and thyme," but I usually leave rosemary out of the dressing. And the best potatoes you will ever eat are small red potatoes, steamed about twenty minutes with butter, salt, and pepper only, and finished with a heaping handful of mixed chives, parsley, and dill. That will get you started using herbs, and you can experiment to discover more.

Q. How do you take care of herbs?

A. Generally speaking, herbs do not like wet feet, so use well-drained soil. During our recent drought years, I have never gone wrong by watering several days a week, and fertilizing at least once a week with a liquid fertilizer for house plants or vegetables. Better soils might not need so much.

When you harvest, cut the thickest stems near the bottom. In fact, cut chives at ground level to insure continued growth. Most of the time you only use the leaves. With rosemary and thyme, pull backwards down the stems to remove the leaves easily. If the stem is so tender that it breaks, then just chop it along with the leaves. For other plants, the leaves will easily pull off.

As a general rule, don't let your herbs bloom. Pinch the buds off as they appear, as well as any leaves or stems that get past their prime and turn yellow. Blossoms will take away from the leaves and will turn some herbs bitter.

Now what is all that advice worth? Well, if you don't live in Florida, it is not worth as much as if you do. If you live in South Florida, it might not be worth much either. For you to be sure my advice will work for you, we have to live in the same place. I am in Zone 9 on all those gardening maps, a zone unto itself. We have frosts and freezes fairly often in December and January, and even as late as April or as early as November. On the other hand, once the nighttime temperatures stay above 72, which can happen in early June, the tomatoes stop setting their blooms, and by late June tomatoes and melons may boil in the afternoon sun.

We all understand that you should think about where you get your advice. I use the Union County (Florida) Extension Office. If you live anywhere else, you shouldn't. As many questions as I get, it seems to me that many people are anxious to receive advice on this subject. Why aren't we that smart with spiritual things? I think the answer is a five letter word—pride. How much sense does that make? Wouldn't it be a shame if that kept us from finding help with things much more important that growing and cooking with herbs?

Consider for a moment, the young teenager who was told that she would give birth to the Son of God. Think about the difficulties she was about to face—perhaps the most difficult ones of telling her parents and her betrothed husband that she was pregnant by the Holy Spirit; even if they believed her, the rest of the community could still count to nine and Gabriel was not likely to visit them all. Where did she immediately turn for support and advice? She went to her older, wiser relative Elizabeth, herself a mother-to-be under miraculous and difficult circumstances. She had already dealt with whispers for six months and became an example of reward after long endurance. They shared faith in a common destiny, evidenced by continuing miracles, including the silence of a miraculously stricken Zacharias. Even at her young age, Mary was wise in choosing to whom she would turn for advice.

On the hand we have Rehoboam, Solomon's son, who, instead of listening to the older wiser counselors who had been there with his father, listened to his young hot-headed friends and wound up losing the majority of his kingdom for it, 1 Kings 12.6–11.

God knew we would need help as we lived our lives. That is one reason he set things up as he did—families with older generations to help the younger, and churches with the wisdom of elders and older brethren. Look for people who have more knowledge of the scriptures than you do. Look for people who have had success, who have come safely through the same trials you are facing, who, in other words, live where you do. God has given us ample help if we will only take advantage of it, so much, in fact, that ignorance will be no excuse. It will simply be a mask for pride.

Aged women likewise be reverent in demeanor, not slanderers nor enslaved to much wine, teachers of that which is good; that they may train the young women to love their husbands, to love their children, to be sober-minded, chaste, workers at home, kind, being in subjection to their own husbands, that the word of God be not blasphemed: the younger men likewise exhort to be sober-minded...likewise, ye younger, be subject unto the elder. Yea, all of you gird yourselves with humility, to serve one another: for God resists the proud, but gives grace to the humble.

Titus 2.3–6; 1 Peter 5.5

28. Trial by Fire

One of my favorite ways to cook vegetables, especially fresh summer vegetables, is to roast them. Cut in similar sized chunks squash, zucchini, sweet peppers, onions, eggplant, and anything else that suits you, carrots, fennel, and leeks maybe, sprinkle with salt and pepper, drizzle with olive oil and roast on a baking sheet at 425 degrees for 30–45 minutes, depending upon your oven and the size chunks you cut. About halfway through, throw in sprigs of fresh marjoram, oregano, rosemary, and thyme, and some minced garlic. Stir every 15 minutes. Yummy!

Without water to dilute the flavor, and with high direct heat to caramelize the outsides, the natural flavor of each vegetable concentrates and sweetens. Dieticians can probably tell you the scientific processes that cause the sugars to creep to the surface and brown, but I don't need a dietician to tell me this is the best way to eat fresh vegetables. And every summer when the garden is producing more than we can possibly keep up with, it is also the healthiest.

A few years ago, a good brother teaching 1 Peter 1.6–7—"if need be you have been put to grief by many trials, that the proof of your faith, being more precious than gold that perishes, though it is proved by fire"—said that when Christians are tried by fire they are "purifried." I think that was a slip of the tongue, but his accidentally coined word has stuck with me ever since.

I used to pray for God to keep my children from trials in their lives, but I got to thinking one day about some of the things we have been through. I bet you have a similar list, things so traumatic at the time you can even put a date on them—September 2, 1988, March 16, 1996, February 22, 2002, February 8, 2005. And that doesn't count the lesser ones—November 1981, June 1984, and so on. Do you know what? We made it through all of them, and we are not the same people today that we would have been if we had never experienced them.

So, to our three precious children, I no longer pray that God will spare you from trials. But I do pray that your faith will be strengthened to see them through, that you will grow as servants of the Lord, and that your wisdom will increase with each experience. As your Mom, I can't help but add, though, "Please, Lord, don't make them *too* hard."

This is the only way to account for passages such as James wrote, "Count it all joy, my brothers, when you fall into many trials; knowing that the proving of your faith works patience, and let patience have its perfect work that you may be perfect and entire, lacking in nothing (1.2–4). Those people understood the value of pain. We all want to lose weight without dieting, slim down and tone up without exercising, grow knowledgeable with studying, but it just won't happen. Nor will growth in faith occur without experiencing some difficulties in life.

How many clichés do we have about this? "No pain, no gain." "When the going gets tough, the tough get going." They are clichés for a reason: they are true. All I have to do is look at my garden and my flower beds. All those carefully tended, watered, and fed plants will die when the drought comes. Those tough old weeds will grow regardless.

As to my roasted vegetables, cooking them under high heat sweetens them. I need to pray that the roasting I undergo will "purifry" me as well.

> *Wherein you greatly rejoice, though now for a little while, if need be, you have been put to grief in manifold trials; that the proof of*

your faith, being more precious than gold that perishes, though it is proved by fire, may be found unto praise and glory and honor at the revelation of Jesus Christ; whom not having seen you love, on whom though now you see him not, yet believing, you rejoice greatly with joy unspeakable and full of glory; receiving the end of your faith, even the salvation of your souls.

1 Peter 1.6–9

29. Pretty Plates

I have never been artistic. The best portrait I ever drew was a stick man. I could make him happy or sad or mad. I could make him hold a shepherd's staff, fish off a pier, or kneel to pray. But I couldn't give him anything more than sticks for arms and legs no matter how hard I tried.

I could never decorate a house. I have friends who can walk into a store, look at a picture or wall hanging and say, "That would look great over the table in the foyer." Would it? I have no idea. Good thing we never had a foyer.

The same is true for my cooking. I could never make anything look like the picture. In fact, my boys learned to judge the taste of things by how ugly they were. If it fell apart on the plate when I served it, they shouted, "Oh boy! This is going to be good!" Food stylists? People who actually make a living making food look artistic? The mere thought of it just confuses me.

I am just as happy to have naturally curly hair. It will only do what it wants to. Saves me a lot of trouble trying to figure out what sort of hairdo would "enhance" my features. Which brings me to the point of all this—true beauty. When a people become so wealthy they can spend thousands on plastic surgery, worry about whether their teeth are white enough, and spend so much time making a plate look "pretty" that the food gets cold, we have become just a little too worried about things that don't really matter.

I came across the passage, "One thing have I asked of Jehovah, that will I seek after; That I may dwell in the house of

Jehovah all the days of my life, To behold the beauty of Jehovah, And to inquire in his temple" (Psa 27.4). So I wondered, what is "the beauty of Jehovah?" It obviously has nothing to do with white teeth, high cheekbones, and hour glass figures. (Hurray!)

It only took a little cross-referencing to find Psalm 63.2–5. Jehovah's power, his glory, and his lovingkindness make him beautiful. Surely there are many other traits, but those certainly stand out from the various "gods" of the people around the Israelites. Petty, tyrannical, cruel, and terrifying well describe the idols the Gentiles worshipped, then and even into the first century. Read the mythology of the Greek gods and you will find the most loathsome characteristics ever attributed to a deity. How could anyone even think of worshipping such things? Yet they did, and actively resisted Jehovah, a God of beautiful character who was not unknown to them.

It makes sense then that his people would be judged by similar things. Deuteronomy 4.6–8 tells us that Israel would be judged as a wise and understanding people, whose God was near them and whose laws were righteous. Are we "beautiful," a people whom God would be pleased to call his own? Are we wise and understanding? Are we righteous? Is God near us, or do we keep him as far away as possible except when we need him? Jesus condemned the Pharisees because they were worried more about the outside than the inside—they made pretty plates, but had ugly insides (Matt 23.25–26).

In general the world is blind to true beauty, whether in a picture, on a plate, or in a person. It makes sense that they would not consider the gospel beautiful either. "Foolishness" Paul says they call it. Just as it takes a hungry man to see the true beauty of a plate of good food, it takes a hungry soul to see the beauty of the gospel. "As it is written, 'How beautiful are the feet of those who preach the good news!'" Paul quotes Isaiah in Romans 10.15. Is that what appeals to you? Or does it have to be some feel good piece of fluff that makes you laugh a lot before it's worth listening to?

One of these days we will see the beauty of Jehovah, His glory and power. I wonder how many will still think it isn't beautiful, but horrifying instead, and only because they never desired to see it in the first place.

> *And even if our gospel is veiled, it is veiled only to those who are perishing. In their case the god of this world has blinded the minds of the unbelievers, to keep them from seeing the light of the gospel of the glory of Christ, who is the image of God.*
>
> 2 Corinthians 4.3–4

30. Authentic Marinara

More than 40 years ago Time-Life put out cookbooks containing authentic recipes from all over the world. I picked up some of them at a used book store in the 70s and several recipes have found a permanent place in my repertoire. From the Chinese book I cook Pepper Steak, Sweet and Sour Pork, and Egg Rolls that are as good as any Chinese restaurant's I have ever had. From the Italian one I use the Pasta Fagioli, the pizza dough and the marinara most often.

That marinara may, in fact, be the recipe I use more than any other. From it I make pizza sauce, spaghetti sauce, and the sauces for eggplant parmagiana, chicken parmagiana, and anything else you can parmagiana. I use it with meatballs, ground beef, and Italian sausage on pasta, and as a dipping sauce for calzones. You can change it up with various herbs and extra vegetables like mushrooms and peppers.

Whenever I serve it, I get remarks like, "Wow! This tastes so—Italian!" Indeed, and why shouldn't it when it is made the way Italians like it—olive oil, onions, garlic, tomatoes, basil, salt and pepper, and a little tomato paste if your tomatoes are extra juicy. It is simple. I can put it together in ten minutes and let it simmer for 30–40 with only a stir here and there. It has thoroughly spoiled my family.

Once, because it was on sale and we were in a hurry, I picked up a canned sauce, one of the better ones as I recall, not simply Ragu. After the first bite, Keith looked at me and said, "What is this? Tomato syrup?" You see, Americans have become so addicted to sugar that nearly all the processed sauces are full of it.

I watched a blind taste test on a television show once, a homemade tomato sauce made by a trained chef, an authentic Italian sauce a whole lot like mine, against a national brand in a jar. The majority preferred the jarred one. They said the homemade one wasn't sweet enough. Why doesn't that make people sit up and take notice? Pasta and sugar? Yuk. It even sounds awful. But that's what Americans want it seems; not the true, authentic sauce, but the syrupy one they have grown accustomed to.

I think the same thing has happened with religion. It doesn't matter to us how the first century church did things. What matters is the hoopla, the spectacle, and the histrionics we have grown accustomed to. If it excites us and makes us feel good, that's what we want. If I can compartmentalize the corporate part of it into a once-every-week-or-so pep rally, and then live as I prefer with no one bothering me about it, then religion has served its purpose.

That religion—mainstream denominational religion—has totally changed its focus. It is nothing but a religion of self. Authentic religion is about God. It wants only what God wants. It lives only for Him and his purpose. It understands that whether I am happy or comfortable or excited has nothing to do with faithfulness. In fact, faithfulness is often shown best when those things are lacking.

Authenticity in religion does matter if you mean to be worshipping someone besides yourself. "I remember the days of old; I meditate on all that you have done; I ponder the work of your hands. I stretch out my hands to you; my soul thirsts for you like a parched land" (Psa 143.5–6). When David was in trouble, when it mattered how God received him—he thought back to the old days. The prophets often told the people to repent and go back to the old ways, the times when they worshipped God truly, instead of pleasing themselves in hedonistic idolatry.

If you find yourself dissatisfied with your religious life, if you see differences in how your group attempts to worship God and how the original Christians did, maybe it's time for you to go on the hunt for some authenticity. Do it before you become addicted to the noise and excitement. It *is* possible to worship in simplicity and truth. It *is* possible to be encouraged by like minded brothers and sisters who want to please God instead of themselves. In the end, they come far closer to the selfless ideal of their Savior than those who are determined to have what they want "because that's how I like it," instead of caring anything at all about how God might like it.

> *Thus says the LORD: "Stand by the roads, and look, and ask for the ancient paths, where the good way is; and walk in it, and find rest for your souls. But they said, 'We will not walk in it.' I set watchmen over you, saying, 'Pay attention to the sound of the trumpet!' But they said, 'We will not pay attention.' Therefore hear, O nations, and know, O congregation, what will happen to them. Hear, O earth; behold, I am bringing disaster upon this people, the fruit of their devices, because they have not paid attention to my words; and as for my law, they have rejected it.*
>
> Jeremiah 6.16–19

31. An Expensive Bowl of Soup

We eat a lot of soup. It's cheap, filling, and healthy. Even a 400 calorie bowlful is a good meal, and most are far less. You won't get tired of it because of the nearly infinite variety.

We have had ham and bean soup, navy bean soup, and white bean and rosemary soup. We've had cream of potato soup, baked potato soup, and *loaded* baked potato soup. I've made bouillabaisse, chicken tortilla, pasta Fagioli, and egg drop soups. For more special occasions I have prepared shrimp bisque, French onion, and vichyssoise. We've warmed our bones with gumbo, mulligatawny, and clam chowder. I've made practically every vegetable soup there is including broccoli cheese soup, roasted tomato soup, and lentil soup. And if you want just plain soup, I have even made chicken noodle. You can have soup every week for a year and not eat the same one twice.

Not only is it cheap to make, it's usually cheap to buy. Often the lowest priced item on a menu is a cup of soup. I can remember it less than a dollar in my lifetime. Even now it's seldom over $3.50. So why in the world would I ever exchange a bowl of soup for something valuable?

By now your mind should have flashed back to Jacob and Esau. Jacob must have been some cook. I have seen the soup he made that day described as everything from lentils to kidney beans to meat stew. It doesn't really matter. It was a simple homespun dish, not even a gourmet concoction of some kind.

Usually people focus on Jacob, tsk-tsk-ing about his conniving and manipulation, but think about Esau today. Yes, he was very tired and hungry after a day's hunt. But was he really going to starve? I've had my men come in from a day of chopping wood and say, "I could eat a horse," but not only did I not feed them one, they would not have eaten it if I had. "I'm starving," is seldom literal.

The Bible makes Esau's attitude plain. After selling his birthright—his double inheritance—for a bowl of soup, Moses writes, "Thus Esau *despised* his birthright" (Gen 25.34). If that inheritance had the proper meaning to him, it would have taken far more than any sort of meal to get it away from him. As it was, that was one expensive bowl of soup!

The Hebrew writer uses another word for Esau—profane: "a profane person such as Esau, who for one mess of meat sold his own birthright" (Heb 12.16). That word means "unholy." It means things pertaining to fleshly existence as opposed to spiritual, things relevant to men rather than God. It is the exact opposite of "sacred" and "sanctified." Jacob understood the value of the birthright, and he also understood his brother's carnal nature. So did God.

What important things are we selling for a mess of pottage? Have you sold your family for the sake of a career? Have you sold your integrity for the sake of wealth? Have you sold your marriage for the sake of a few "I told you so's?" Have you sold your place in the body of Christ for a few opinions? Have you sold your soul for the pleasure you can have here and now?

Examine your life today, the things you have settled for instead of working for, the things you have given up and the things you gave them up for. Have you made some really bad deals? Can you even recognize the true value of what you have lost? Don't despise the blessings God has given you. Don't sell your family, or your character, or your soul for a bowl of soup.

Brothers, join in imitating me, and keep your eyes on those who walk according to the example you have in us. For many, of whom I have often told you and now tell you even with tears, walk as enemies of the cross of Christ. Their end is destruction, their god is their belly, and they glory in their shame, with minds set on earthly things. But our citizenship is in heaven, and from it we await a Savior, the Lord Jesus Christ

Philippians 3.17–20

32. Shelf Life

I never thought about sodas having a shelf life until a couple of years ago. We bought several boxes at a great sale and stacked them out of the way until needed. We put one on the floor of the pantry back behind the potatoes, onions, and other odds and ends that won't fit on a shelf. It takes us two or three months to go through one 12 pack, so by the time we had finished the first few, we had totally forgotten about that one. I only found it because I dropped something that rolled into the back of the pantry and had to pull everything out to find it.

We decided to celebrate our discovery with a soda. It wasn't just flat. It was the worst thing I ever put in my mouth. On a whim, we searched the box, and sure enough, there was a sell-by date that was about a year past.

We all have shelf lives too, as much as we hate to think about it. But instead of viewing this from the perspective of immortality—how short our lives really are—we seem to view it from the perspective of the shelf life of a bottle of milk—compared to that we live practically forever. Maybe that is why we view death as a tragedy instead of a victory. We keep looking through the wrong end of the binoculars. One of the most difficult things we have to do as Christians is constantly changing our perspectives, re-focusing our hearts from things in plain sight to things which the world cannot, and will not, see.

Second Chronicles 34 and 35 tell us the story of Josiah, the last good king of Judah. He tried to clean up a Temple that was in disrepair and a worship that was in disarray. As his *reward*

God said he would not live to see destruction brought upon Judah. What!? Dying was a reward? Yes, because this godly man had his perspective correct. He viewed going on to the next life as far preferable to seeing God's people destroyed.

Josiah died in battle at the age of 39. Dying young was his *reward* for faithfulness. What one of us would not look at that fact superficially and say, "What a tragedy for such a good man to die so young?" Maybe I need to rethink my attitude about death. I may grieve, but faith means my life will not be ruined by the death of a loved one. I may have a little concern about how it will be to die, but faith means I should not be terrified.

I hope I am not coming across as morbid. Maybe having nearly become a relatively young widow twice in eight years has me more aware of the possibilities these days. I simply mean to remind us that we have hopes and comforts the rest of the world doesn't.

I have a shelf life and so do you. It is shorter than we think, and it will mean nothing to us in that first glimpse of Eternity. I imagine we will be glad to be there, and wonder why we worried even a little.

> *For me to live is Christ and to die is gain. …I am in a strait between the two, having the desire to depart and be with Christ, for it is far better.*
>
> Philippians 1.21, 23

33. Gravy

My family loves gravy. I would never think of serving bare rice or naked mashed potatoes. There must always be gravy.

On the other hand, sometimes you cannot have gravy. When you grill a steak, there is no gravy. When you smoke a chicken quarter, there is no gravy, and if somehow you did catch the drippings, you wouldn't want them. Believe me, I tried it once. Smoked drippings simply taste bitter. Oh, you can always fake it with butter, flour, and canned broth, but any gravy connoisseur will know the difference. You only get really good gravy with fresh meat drippings, flour sizzled in the pan, and a liquid of your choice.

Yet, if your life depended upon it, you would choose the meat over the gravy any time. You would know that the only real nutritional value, the only real protein, is in the meat and not the gravy. If you tried to live on nothing but gravy alone, you would soon starve. You might be round as a beach ball, but you would still starve.

Too many times we give up the meat for the gravy. We give up marriages and families for the sake of career and money. We give up a spiritual family that will help us no matter what for fair weather friends who won't. We even give up our souls for the sake of good times, status, and convenience.

Then there are the times when it seems like life makes no gravy. So we give up God because he dared to allow something less than ease, comfort, and fun into our lives. Can't have the gravy too? Then I don't want you, Lord. You're going to give up a grilled rib eye because it doesn't come with gravy? Really?

I doubt we realize exactly what we are doing. The problem is that we have things reversed. We think this life is the meat, and the next is just the gravy. That is what we are saying when we give up on God because things didn't turn out so well here. Justin Martyr, a philosopher who was converted to Christianity in the early half of the second century wrote, "*Since our thoughts are not fixed on the present*, we are not concerned when men put us to death. Death is a debt we must all pay anyway" (*First Apology*, chapter 11).

Can we say that, or are we too addicted to our pleasure loving, wealthy culture? The first Christians converted with the knowledge that they would probably lose everything they owned and die within a matter of weeks, if not days. And us? We are out there looking for the gravy and blaming God for his scanty menu.

The fact is we do have some gravy promised in this life. We just look for it in the wrong places. "Then Peter said in reply, 'See, we have left everything and followed you. What then will we have?' Jesus said to them… everyone who has left houses or brothers or sisters or father or mother or children or lands, for my name's sake, will receive a hundredfold and will inherit eternal life" (Matt 19.27, 29). Are you still looking to the world for your gravy? Jesus plainly says the place to look is in your spiritual family. When it works as he intended—*even if it only comes close*—it is far better than anything the world will ever offer you.

So remember where to find your spiritual sustenance. Remember where to go when times are rough and you need a hand. And even those things are not the meat. The meat is eternal life with a Creator who loved you enough to die.

Everything else is just gravy.

Train yourself for godliness; for while bodily training is of some value, godliness is of value in every way, as it holds promise for the present life and also for the life to come.

1 Timothy 4.7–8

34. Bread Crumbs

Have you discovered *panko* yet? *Panko* is Japanese bread crumbs, an extra light variety that cooks up super-crunchy on things like crab cakes and shrimp. They also cost more than regular bread crumbs, but in certain applications they are worth it. On the other hand a chicken or veal Milanese needs a sturdier crumb to stand up to the lemony butter sauce, an oven fried pork chop needs melba toast crumbs that will cook to a crunch without burning in a high heat oven, and my favorite broccoli casserole needs the faint sweetness of a butter cracker crumb to really set it off.

Although none of these dishes are the food of poverty, using the crumbs and crusts of food rather than tossing them out certainly grew out of the necessity of using whatever was at hand to feed hungry bellies for thousands of years, and now we all do it, even when there is plenty in the pantry. Pies and cheesecakes with graham cracker crumb crusts, anyone? Dressing to stuff your poultry? Bread pudding on a cold winter night? Streusel on that warm coffee cake in the morning? Bread-infused peasant food has even shown up on gourmet cooking shows in the form of panzanella (salad) and ribolita (soup), both of which use chunks of stale bread to bolster their ability to satisfy appetites.

That reminds me of a woman 2,000 years ago who understood the value of leftovers. Her little daughter was demon-possessed, so ill she could not travel, but her mother had heard of someone who might be able to help, who even then was in hiding from the crowds on the border of her country. It took a lot for her to seek him out, first leaving her sick child in some-one else's care, then approaching this Jewish rabbi, a type who had either reviled or ignored her all her life; but a desperate mother will make any sacrifice to save her child.

Sure enough, even though she addressed him by the Messianic title, "Son of David," he *answered her not a word* (Matt 15.22–23). Still she persisted, and this time she was insulted—he called her a dog. Oh, he was nicer about it than most, using the Greek word for "little pet dog," *kunarion,* rather than the epithet she usually heard from his kind—*kuno,* ownerless scavenging dogs that run wild in the streets, but still he made her inequality in his eyes obvious.

This woman, though, was ready to accept his judgment of her: *Even the dogs get the crumbs, sir.* Moreover, she understood that was all she needed. This man, whose abilities she had heard of from afar, was more than just a man, and even the tiniest morsel of his power was enough to heal her child, even from a distance.

Do we understand that? Do we realize that one drop of God's power can fix any problem we have, and more, do we have the humility to accept our place in His plan, even if it is not what we have planned? Yes, every day I ask for more—more grace, more faith, more of His power to change me and use me, but do I really comprehend His strength? I would say it was impossible to do so, except for the example of this desperate Gentile mother who, like a widow of her nation hundreds of years before her, had more faith, trust, and humility than the religious men of God's chosen people (1 Kgs 17; Luke 4.25–26).

And for this, perhaps, God chose her to foreshadow in the Son's life the crumbling of the barrier between Jew and Gentile, and the inclusive nature of the gospel which had been foretold from the beginning: "in thy seed shall *all* nations of the earth be blessed" (Gen 22.17).

Do I have the faith and humility to accept God's plan for me? One thing is certain—this Gentile mother knew she had nowhere else to turn, and neither do we.

Even God's crumbs are enough to satisfy our every need.

For this cause I bow my knees to the Father... that you... may be strong to apprehend with all the saints what is the breadth and length and height and depth, and to know the love of Christ which passes knowledge, that you may be filled with all the fullness of God...him who is able to do exceeding abundantly above all that we ask or think.

Ephesians 3.14, 17–20

35. My Most Embarrassing Moments

A cooking magazine I read used to run a page of embarrassing mistakes its readers had made in the kitchen. I probably could have kept the page going for several years single-handedly.

I tend to become flustered when I have company. We had an older couple over for Sunday dinner once, sweet, kind people whom I should never have been nervous about at all. Everything was going well as I slid my homemade crescent rolls into the oven. Twelve minutes later I peeked in to see how they were doing and was horrified. I had covered them with a linen kitchen towel during their last rise and had forgotten to take it off.

I pulled them out, managed to remove the towel without mutilating my rolls, and slid them back in, but the damage was already done. They never did fully rise, instead becoming heavy and doughy and tasting faintly of freshly ironed cotton. "I thought maybe it was a new-fangled method I hadn't heard about before," said my sweet friend. Indeed—a new-fangled method that did not work very well at all.

Then there was the time I put a ten pound ham in the oven and very carefully set the oven timer backwards. Instead of starting at 10:00 and cooking till 12:30, it was rigged to come on at 12:30 and cook till 10:00. My twelve guests and I walked in at 12:15 to a stone cold ham. Aren't microwaves wonderful? I sliced off enough to go around once, zapped them, and called everyone to the table while the rest finished nuking. At least I had managed to get everything else done on time.

And who could forget the first meal I cooked for Keith after our honeymoon? I pulled the meat loaf out of the oven, holding that brand new Pyrex loaf pan between those slick new oven mitts. I turned around a bit too quickly and, as I did, that pan slid out of my grasp and sailed across the room landing upside down in the floor behind the table. Keith managed to duck, but it was a portentous way to begin married life.

Yet all those embarrassing moments, and many, many others, are stories we laugh about now. In fact, most of them we were laughing about the same day, often within minutes of their occurrence. Look how well-balanced we are. No arrogance here, no stubborn pride. We can learn from our mistakes, even laugh at ourselves.

But let one person dare to disagree with us about a spiritual matter and that's a completely different story. Our minds are made up; we won't listen; we instantly dismiss any scriptural evidence we cannot otherwise explain away with, "That's different."

Let anyone dare to tell us we might have erred in our actions and things are even worse. Instantly we counterattack; instantly we rationalize; instantly we blame that person for our failure to behave as a Christian. If he had told us differently, we would have listened. Really now?

I can hear you and yes, you are right—these are *not* laughing matters, but that makes it even more important that we *not* get too angry to listen, or too "hurt" to examine ourselves objectively. I can tell tales about my mistakes in the kitchen over and over, but heaven forbid (or is it some other place?) I actually consider another side to a disagreement or scrutinize my own actions and their motives.

Why can't we share stories of change and enlightenment in spiritual matters? Why can't we thank the ones who told us we were wrong instead of telling everyone else how horrible they are? Why is it that the very thing we say all the time, "I know I'm not perfect," is the last thing we will ever admit?

Perhaps it's because we don't really believe it.

> *He is in the way of life who heeds correction; but he who forsakes reproof errs. …He who hearkens to the reproof of life shall abide among the wise. He who refuses correction despises his own soul; but he who hearkens to reproof gets understanding.*

Proverbs 10.17; 15.31–32

36. What I Did On My Summer Vacation

The garden has come and gone in the past six weeks. Day after hot, humid day I stood in the kitchen, scalding, blanching, peeling, seeding, chopping, mixing, packing, freezing, pickling, preserving and canning. After an hour or more in the garden, followed by six hours of standing in the kitchen, my back ached, my feet throbbed, and I had a knot between my shoulders blades. Then the next day I got up and did it again. In the evenings we shelled and snapped until midnight or our hands ached too much to continue, whichever came first.

So why did I do it? Because it had to be done. This is one way we manage not only to survive on what we make, but to eat fairly well in spite of what we make. This is how we fed two teenage boys and remained financially solvent. And it wasn't all bad.

Some days I managed to do a lot of meditating while I worked. When you must do the same action over and over, like peeling four hundred tomatoes, it becomes automatic, so you can use your mind for better things, pondering recent lessons you have heard, drawing conclusions from verses you have read, and praying through some of the problems that beset you.

Keith took a few days off during all this to help me out. I am not quite what I used to be, and the live-in help left quite a few years ago. We cannot "chat" over our work as most couples can. Sometimes I touched his arm to get his attention so I could tell him something I thought important. Other times he spoke (since I don't have to see to hear) and then I could reply when he looked up. Once or twice we got into a friendly competition. He still cannot fill a jar as quickly as I can—his hands are bigger and not as well trained, but what he could do still meant jars I did not have to fill myself. And even after thirty-eight years, or more probably because of them, it was pleasant to be together.

The other day Lucas said something like, "Isn't it funny how we look forward to the garden starting, and then near the end look forward to it ending?" And he is right—except for the chili peppers and the grapes, things are nearly at an end, and I am glad. Still, at the end of each day's work the past month, I looked on the rows of jars cooling on an old rag of a towel laid across the countertop and felt a sense of accomplishment, despite the occasional tedium, the many aches, and the pools of sweat on the floor from the rising steam in the kitchen.

I wish you could see my pantry—23 jars of tomatoes, 15 jars of salsa, 18 jars of dill pickles, a dozen jars each of okra dills and pickled banana pepper rings, and 30 jars of three kinds of jellies and jams. Then open the freezer—two dozen bags of corn, 20 bags of green beans, ten bags of lima beans, eight bags of zipper cream peas, 12 quarts of tomato sauce, and eight quarts of blueberries. The best is yet to come though, when my grocery bill totals half what it might have been and ultimately, when we eat it all.

So maybe it was not what some might consider a "summer vacation." In fact, I also had a couple of days worth of testing at the eye clinic mixed in there somewhere, but it was a worthwhile venture that did us far more good than tanning at a beach might have.

I think living a Christian life might be the same sort of vacation. Some days it is hard work. Some days it is tedious. Some days it causes us pain. But we can make even the worst days better by meditating on the comfort in God's word, and by talking to Him whenever we want to. We have a spiritual family who will help bear our burdens, who will weep when we weep and rejoice when we rejoice, people who will make the bad days go quicker and the good days even happier.

And then before you know it, it's almost over. But there are things we can look back on with satisfaction, unlike our friends in the world who will have so much to regret. They will also have nothing to look forward to, while for us the best is yet to come, and aren't we looking forward to that?

For all of us summer will soon turn to fall, and after that the winter. Make sure your pantry is full.

And I heard the voice from heaven saying, Write, Blessed are the dead who die in the Lord from henceforth, yes, says the Spirit, that they may rest from their labors, for their works follow with them.

Revelation 14.13

37. Popcorn

Popcorn is our snack of choice when watching ball games. We make it the old fashioned way—bacon grease in a large saucepan, bulk popcorn from a large plastic bag, and salt. Heat it over high heat, shaking the pan until it stops popping. The stuff out of the microwave cannot begin to compare.

We still wind up with what the industry calls "old maids," kernels that have not popped. Usually it's the kernel's fault, not the popper's.

They tell me that popcorn kernels are the only grain with a hard moisture-proof hull. That means that not only can moisture not get into the kernel, but the moisture inside the kernel cannot get out either. As you heat them, the steam inside increases until the pressure reaches 135 PSI and the heat 180 degrees Celsius (356 for us non-scientists). At that point, the starch inside the kernel gelatinizes, becoming soft and pliable. When the hull explodes the steam expands the starch and proteins into the airy foam we know as popcorn.

I found two theories about old maids. One is that there is not enough moisture in the kernel to begin with; the other is that the hull develops a leak, acting as a release valve so that pressure cannot build enough for the "explosion." Either way, the kernels just sit there and scorch, becoming harder and drier as they cook.

Isn't that what happens when we undergo trials? Some of us use the experience to flower into a stronger, wiser, more pleasant personality. Others of us sit there and scorch in the heat until we dry up completely, no use for God or His people, let alone ourselves. The resulting bitterness is reflected in the cynical way we view the world, the way we continue to wallow in the misery of our losses, and the impenetrable barrier we raise whenever anyone tries to help us. As Israel said when they had forsaken God for idols and knew they would be punished, "Our bones have dried up, our hope is lost, we are clean cut off" (Ezek 37.11). When we refuse to seek God in our day of trouble, when we forget the blessings He has given us even though we deserved none, that is the result.

But God can help even the hopeless. He can bring us back from despair. He can make our hearts blossom in the heat of trial if we remember the lesson about priorities, about what really counts in the end. "If we have only hoped in Christ in this life, we are of all men most pitiable" (1 Cor 15.19), and that is exactly where we find ourselves if we allow anything in this life to steal our faith in God.

Trials are not pleasant; they are not meant to be. They are meant to create something new in us, something stronger and more spiritual. When, instead, we become hard and bitter, we are like the old maids in a bag of popcorn, and when the popcorn fizzles, it's the popcorn's fault.

For our light affliction, which is for the moment, works for us more and more exceedingly an eternal weight of glory; while we look not at the things which are seen, but at the things which are not seen: for the things which are seen are temporal; but the things which are not seen are eternal.

2 Corinthians 4.17–18

38. Calzones

I had invited a couple of friends for lunch. One in particular had been raving about a calzone I made for her a couple of years before. So I promised her another. I had bought everything from memory. With the price of gas making one trip to town cost $8, I buy everything I need for the week on one day.

Suddenly in the middle of the night I woke up and said to myself, "Cheese!" I had forgotten the mozzarella and provolone. How in the world can you even think of making what is basically a pizza turnover and forget the cheese? It's like planning to make brownies and forgetting the chocolate!

We are no better when we try to be children of God and forget the basic elements.

The Pharisees thought that since they tithed even their herb seeds, they were good Jews. They were certainly right to be so careful. "Every tithe of the land, whether of the seed of the land or of the fruit of the trees, is the LORD's; it is holy to the LORD. You shall tithe all the yield of your seed that comes from the field year by year" (Lev 27.30; Deut 14.22). Yet Jesus reminded them that they had left out "the weightier matters of the law, justice, mercy, and faithfulness" (Matt 23.23). How did they think they could be children of a just and merciful God and leave those things out? It should have been unthinkable.

John dealt with people who thought they could be followers of Christ and live immoral lives. He was plain about their mistaken ideas. "Whoever says 'I know him' but does not keep his commandments is a liar, and the truth is not in him" (1 John

2.4). He reminded them of the same thing Jesus reminded the Pharisees. How can you think you are a child of God if you don't live by his rules? "No one born of God makes a practice of sinning, for God's seed abides in him, and he cannot keep on sinning because he has been born of God. By this it is evident who are the children of God, and who are the children of the devil: whoever does not practice righteousness is not of God, nor is the one who does not love his brother" (1 John 3.9–10). I don't know about you, but I get really tired of famous athletes who wear crosses around their necks and "thank Jesus" before the cameras, but live like the Devil otherwise.

It's time for all of us to stop trying to make calzones without the cheese. You can't pick and choose which commandments you want to follow and then claim to be an obedient and faithful child of God.

Children do not tell their parents which of the house rules they will and will not obey. They are obedient to the parents in all things, and they understand that being a child of their own particular parents means certain things simply are or are not done if they want to stay faithful to the values of that home. How many of us have said, "Your mother would roll over in her grave if she saw you do that?" We understand what faithfulness to the spirit of the parent means, even if some specific idea is not spelled out in black and white. Why are we so dense when we come to our dealings with God?

The next time you make your family's favorite dish, using every single ingredient because you would hate to disappoint them, remember not to disappoint God either.

*Religion that is pure and undefiled before God, the Father, is this: to visit the orphans and widows in their affliction, **and** to keep oneself unstained from the world.*

James 1.27

39. Reading Recipes

After reading them for so many years, I can skim a recipe and garner all sorts of necessary information in that quick once-over. Not just whether I have the ingredients, but how long it will take, what I can do ahead of time, what equipment I will need, the substitutions I can make if necessary, and whether I can cut it in half or freeze half of it. Sometimes, though, a recipe needs a closer reading.

I made a vegetable lasagna once that turned out well, but way too big. I took over half of the leftovers to my women's class potluck and it got rave reviews and several requests. So I went home and started typing the two page recipe containing at least two dozen ingredients. The typing required a careful reading of the recipe so I wouldn't give anyone wrong amounts or directions, and as I did so I discovered that I had completely forgotten one ingredient and had missed one of the procedures. Just imagine how good it would have been if I had done the whole thing correctly.

Too many times we try to read the Bible like I read that recipe, especially the passages we think we already know. I have said many times to many classes, the biggest hindrance to learning is what you *think* you already know. Today I am going to prove it to you.

Have you ever said, or even taught, that turning the water to wine was the first miracle Jesus ever did? I know, it's what all the Bible class curricula say. Well, it's your job to check out those lessons with your own careful reading. Most of the time that means reading far beyond the actual lesson text. This isn't even hard to see, but you do have to think about what you see. Some time today when you have the time—okay, *make* the time—read the following verses.

> John 1.45–51, Jesus tells Nathanael that he saw him before it was possible for him to see him. This was enough of a miracle that it brought a confession from Nathanael: "Rabbi, you are the Son of God, you are the King of Israel" (v 49)
>
> 2.11, "This is the first of his signs" (water to wine)
>
> 2.23, "Now when he was in Jerusalem at the Passover Feast, many believed on his name when they saw the signs that he was doing" (Notice, this is an unknown number of signs)
>
> 4.16–19, Jesus tells the woman at the well all about her life, a life he could not have known about except miraculously. She would later tell her neighbors, "Come see a man who told me all that ever I did. Can this be the Christ?" (v 29). She certainly thought she had seen a miracle.
>
> 4.46–54, Jesus heals the nobleman's son, which John labels "the second sign that Jesus did." What about John 1? What about 2.23? What about Samaria?

For years I read "first" and "second," knowing full well about the other signs before and between them, and didn't even think about what I was reading. I was reading it like a recipe, a quick once over because I already knew the story. Now having seen all the passages together you can see that "first" and "second" in John 2.11 and 4.54 obviously do not mean the simple chronological "first" and "second" you might think at first glance. You need the entire context of John to figure it out.

"Now Jesus did many other signs in the presence of the disciples, which are not written in this book; but these are written so that you may believe that Jesus is the Christ, the Son of God, and that by believing you may have life in his name" (John 20.30–31). Right there John tells you not only why he wrote his book, but that he simply chose certain signs to discuss in detail.

If you do a careful study of the entire book, you will discover that he chose seven, each making a particular point about the power of Jesus that proves his Deity. No, I am not going to list them for you. You need to take up your Bibles and figure it out for yourself so you know firsthand.

When John says "This is the first," and "this is the second," he is simply referring to the list of seven he intends to discuss more fully. Turning the water to wine was the first on his list, *not* the first miracle Jesus ever did, and all you have to do is read earlier in the book to see at least one more—Nathanael's. In fact, you cannot even count the number he did in between the "first" and the "second" (2.23).

So, be careful what you believe. Be even more careful what you teach because that could affect many others. Pay attention to the details and don't pull events and verses out of context. Do you want to know why so many false doctrines spread? Because people read the "proof texts" like a recipe, a quick scan instead of a careful reading, if indeed they read them at all.

Don't skim the Word of God. Give it the attention it deserves.

> *And we have something more sure, the prophetic word, to which you will do well to pay attention as to a lamp shining in a dark place, until the day dawns and the morning star rises in your hearts.*

> 2 Peter 1.19

40. Comfort Food

Do a little research and you will find that the term "comfort food" was added to Webster's Dictionary in 1972. It refers to foods that are typically inexpensive, uncomplicated, and require little or no preparation at all; foods which usually bring pleasant associations with childhood, just as an old song can remind one of a long ago romance, or a smell can instantly bring back situations both good and bad.

Comfort foods vary from culture to culture, but in our country usually include things like macaroni and cheese, mashed potatoes, fried chicken, ice cream, peanut butter, and brownies. Folks tend to use comfort foods to provide familiarity and emotional security, or to reward themselves. It's not surprising that many of these are loaded with carbohydrates which can produce a soporific effect as well. Comfort food followed closely by the comfort of sleep.

Since it became fashionable I have tried to figure out my own list of comfort foods. Here is my problem: my mother was such a good cook and so adventurous, trying many recipes day after day, that I never had one dish often enough to form an attachment to it. One cooking magazine actually runs the column, "My Mother's Best Meal." I could not possibly pick one. I would need a whole page to list them. So for me it isn't comfort food, it's comfort cooking. When my mind is in turmoil, I cook all day long, trying, I suppose, to recreate the warm, homey, safe atmosphere of my mother's kitchen.

Comfort food works for the soul too. The best part is, you

don't have to be a good cook. You just open the word of God and feast. You turn on the water of life and drink to your heart's content. You produce the fruit of the lips in praise to God whenever and wherever you desire. You gather with your brothers and sisters and wallow in a fellowship that has absolutely nothing to do with coffee and donuts.

You can get fatter and fatter with all that spiritual nourishment and still be healthy. In fact, in this context at least, the skinnier you are, the sicker, the sadder, and the weaker you are.

So grab a spoon today, and everyday, and dig in.

Work not for the food which perishes, but for the food which abides unto eternal life, which the Son of man shall give unto you: for him the Father, even God, has sealed.

John 6.27

41. Please Pass the Salt

Keith and I have differing opinions about salt. He adds it to everything, copiously. I add it to some things all the time and others seldom, and usually just a mere sprinkle. Since his stroke a few years ago, he has become a little more moderate, using "Lite Salt" instead of regular table salt, and cutting his amounts by using serious quantities of black pepper instead.

In the summer he must worry less about it. We live in Florida, which means on a summer afternoon he will come in from the garden soaking wet, with his pant hems literally dripping sweat. He stays hydrated with a gallon of water sitting in the shade of a nearby oak, usually a gallon before lunch and another afterward. On those days, he doesn't worry about how much salt he puts on his platter of sliced garden tomatoes in the evening.

Just out of curiosity I looked up the dietary salt requirement. Considering how much you hear about the evils of salt, I was surprised. Did you know that too little in your diet can affect your moods and even cause depression? It is also the reason for some falls in the elderly. They wind up with hyponatremia, which causes dizziness and balance issues. Low salt diets can lead to Type 2 diabetes by impairing insulin sensitivity. None of this gives us the green light to eat too much salt, but maybe we should check where we stand with our doctors on these issues before cutting out too much salt.

In all that study I also found a list of special uses for salt. We all know that salt is a food preservative. I also use it as a gargle for sore throats. I hate doing it, but it works. These other things I have not tried, so take them with, ahem, a grain of salt.

Sprinkle salt on the shelves in your pantry to keep away the ants.

Soak freshly caught fish in salt water to make scaling them easier.

A pinch of salt in egg whites will make them beat up fluffier.

A dash of salt in gelatin will cause it to set faster.

Clean greens in salt water for easier dirt removal.

Pour salt on an ink-stained carpet and leave overnight. It will soak up the stain.

Pour salt on sidewalk cracks to kill weeds and grass.

Then I looked up salt in the scriptures and got another education.

Ezekiel 16.4 mentions rubbing a newborn with salt. For some that symbolized cleansing. For the Eastern cultures at large, it was thought to make the infant's skin firm.

Exodus 30.35 and Leviticus 2.13 tell us that God *required* salt on his sacrifices. Salt was considered the opposite of leavening (so much for the notion that no salt should be used in unleavened bread), and it signified both the purity and faithfulness required to worship Jehovah, and also Jehovah's enduring love for his people.

And that led to the "covenants of salt" mentioned in places like Numbers 18.19 and 2 Chronicles 13.5. God's covenant with his people was considered perpetual.

So now you see why I started looking at Colossians 4.6 a little differently: "Let your speech always be gracious, seasoned with salt, so that you may know how to answer each person." Usually I hear, "Salt makes things sweeter, so be sweet and kind when you talk with someone." That is truly a one-dimensional explanation. Yes, salt can make a tasteless melon taste sweeter. Even the ancients knew that (Job 6.6). One of the classic combinations in Italian cooking is prosciutto, a salty ham, thinly sliced and wrapped around melon wedges. Yet if there is no sugar in the food, the salt can hardly make it taste sweeter. The correct statement is that salt brings out whatever flavors are present in the first place.

And what about the other aspects of salt associated with that culture, purification, preservation, faithfulness, and perpetuality? That verse in Colossians indicates that my answer may change according to circumstance, "that you may know how to answer *each* person." Can the words I choose help purify a sinner? Can they show my faithfulness to God when I am questioned by an unbeliever? Can they tell others that I *know* my God will always be there for me and that is why I will always be there for him, regardless how they treat me? Absolutely, and some of those words might not be particularly sweet.

Salt, on occasion, stings. So does God's grace when it offers me things I do not want to hear in my present circumstances, so my "graciousness" to others may well have them smarting when it comes "out of season"—a time they do not want to hear it. In fact, since salt can only enhance what is already there, perhaps it is the hearer who determines how sweet my words are in the first place.

God's Word is simple enough for anyone to understand it on the surface, but remember that if you apply yourself, you can dig deeper into more layers than in any book written by a man. Salt, for instance, can flavor your studies for a good while.

> *You are the salt of the earth, but if salt has lost its taste, how shall its saltiness be restored? It is no longer good for anything except to be thrown out and trampled under people's feet.*
>
> Matthew 5.13

42. The Garbage Can

We had a terrible time with gnats this past summer. Despite our automatic atomizer, a dozen swarmed the lights at night and several buzzed us during dinner. So I looked up the breeding habits of gnats and found out why. We live in a veritable breeding ground—standing water (water buckets for the dogs), damp landscaping (mulch in the flower beds and more rain last year than any in the past ten), food (a large vegetable garden, a blueberry patch, and grape vines), and, ahem, animal residue— we live in the country, it's everywhere.

So keeping the doors and windows shut should fix the problem, right? No, they breed in garbage cans too. When you live in the country there is no weekly pickup. You must carry your garbage and trash to the dump. To minimize the number of trips we put all the flammable items in a paper bag to burn in the "burn barrel" onsite, and the wet garbage in the kitchen can until it fills enough to empty it into the one outside. That means our kitchen can is probably emptied less often than yours because there is no paper trash "filler," and that means plenty of time for any gnats that whiz in a door as we enter or leave to lay eggs and hatch. I have tried spraying it every morning with insecticide, but even that does not seem to help.

There is no getting around it. Garbage breeds vermin of one sort or another all the time. They simply love filth. Putting it in the garbage can, as long as the can is still inside the house, doesn't really help a bit. You have to remove it from the house entirely, and soon enough that the gnats cannot breed.

If we don't want spiritual vermin, we have to get rid of the garbage in our hearts. It doesn't help to just try to hide it. "Make no provision for the flesh, to fulfill the lusts thereof" Paul told the Roman brethren (13.14). You can't just stash it away in case you might want to indulge again. You have to remove it completely, and soon enough that it doesn't breed yet more. The Devil loves the dirt. His minions wallow in it. Why do we think it won't soil us too as long as no one knows? Would you eat a meal that was swarming with gnats and flies?

Get rid of the gnats in your soul. The only way is to empty that garbage can inside yourself and keep it that way.

Touch no unclean thing and I will receive you. And I will be to you a father and you shall be to me sons and daughters, says the Lord Almighty. Having therefore these promises, beloved, let us therefore cleanse ourselves from all filthiness of flesh and spirit, perfecting holiness in the fear of God.

2 Corinthians 6.17–7.1

43. Chemistry in the Kitchen

Cooking is a funny thing. Sometimes you can mess around with it and sometimes you can't. My recipe for minestrone is not something a purist would recognize as minestrone, and it's never the same. Some of it depends upon what's in the refrigerator, and some of it comes from our likes and dislikes. You can change it around, but as long as it winds up as a brothy soup with a bunch of vegetables in it, some kind of pasta, and some Mediterranean herbs, you can call it minestrone. You really can't mess it up unless you do something just plain weird with it, like pouring in a bottle of molasses.

Baking is another matter. You must think long and hard before you change anything in a recipe for baked goods. If you don't, it can fall, or not rise, or be too dry to choke down, or so "short" that it turns into crumbs when you touch it. If you use baking soda, you must have an acid like buttermilk or sour cream. If you get any fat in your egg whites they won't whip. If you don't heat the liquid, your yeast won't rise, but if you heat it too much you kill it. Baking is chemistry and it does make a difference.

A lot of people don't want to follow any sort of recipe in their religion. They think it is about good hearts, sincere love, and feeling good, none of which is quantifiable, and therefore none of which can be legislated. They will proclaim that the early church did things differently depending upon the location and the culture, and in some cases they are correct. Just like cooking minestrone can be varied according to the ingredients on hand and the palates of the eaters. But sometimes it is like baking—it does make a difference if you don't want your cake to fall.

The word may not be used in the New Testament, but the concept of an appropriate orthodoxy is there in black and white.

> And when they had appointed elders for them *in every church,* with prayer and fasting they committed them to the Lord in whom they had believed. (Acts 14.23)

> That is why I sent you Timothy, my beloved and faithful child in the Lord, to remind you of my ways in Christ, *as I teach them everywhere in every church.* (1 Cor 4.17)

> Only let each person lead the life that the Lord has assigned to him, and to which God has called him. *This is my rule in all the churches.* (1 Cor 7.17)

> For God is not a God of confusion but of peace. *As in all the churches of the saints.* (1 Cor 14.33)

> Now concerning the collection for the saints: as I directed the churches of Galatia, *so you also are to do.* (1 Cor 16.1)

There are certain things the apostles expected to be done everywhere. The methods were not always specified, and that's where we get to choose our ingredients, but the other things are religious "baking"—things that must be done for our service to God to be acceptable. If we think we can change the chemistry we are wrong. Put egg whites in a greasy bowl and they will not turn into a beautiful meringue no matter how sincerely you beat them.

As you can plainly see from the passages quoted above, God expects some control over our service to him. Some folks chafe at the idea that we cannot change anything and everything about our religious service at our own whims. Israel had the same problem and wound up in Babylonian captivity. Don't make the mistakes they did.

> *He will render to each one according to his works: to those who by patience in well-doing seek for glory and honor and immortality, he will give eternal life; but for those who are self-seeking and do not obey the truth, but obey unrighteousness, there will be wrath and fury.*

> Romans 2.6–8

44. Leftovers

After a holiday meal we eat a lot of leftovers—turkey pot pie, turkey divan, turkey enchiladas, turkey soup, turkey salad, and anything else that will use up a good-sized portion of that leftover bird. It seems they all have something in common—some sort of sauce, gravy, or broth to make the endlessly heated up, dried out meat palatable. If you like turkey leftovers, it is not the turkey you like—it is what the turkey becomes, a new dish with flavorful moist ingredients that fill you up and satisfy your hunger. You can only reheat unadorned meat, particularly low fat meat or poultry, so many times before it turns into sawdust.

While my family enjoys leftover turkey dishes, God most emphatically does not like leftovers.

If you are a gardener, you understand the concept of first-fruits. The first pickings, like the first serving of turkey, are always the best. By the end of the summer the beans are tough, the corn is starchy, the squash is wormy, and the tomatoes are small and hard or half-rotten. That is why you doll them up in casseroles and sauces. I always make the tomato sauce in July. The June tomatoes are ripe, sweet and juicy, far too good to turn into sauce.

God has always expected the first-fruits from His people. "The first of the first-fruits of your ground you shall bring into the house of Jehovah your God" (Exod 23.19). He expected the first-fruits of everything to be given to His servants, the priests, who waited on Him night and day, "And this shall be the priests' due from the people, from them that offer a sacrifice, whether it be ox or sheep, that they shall give unto the priest the shoulder, and the two cheeks, and the maw. The first-fruits of your grain, of your new wine, and of your oil, and the first of the fleece of your sheep, shall you give him" (Deut 18.3–4).

The Israelites in Malachi's day discovered exactly how God felt about offerings that were less than the best. "You offer polluted bread upon my altar. And you say, Wherein have we polluted you? In that you say, The table of Jehovah is contemptible. And when you offer the blind for sacrifice, it is no evil! And when you offer the lame and sick, it is no evil! Present it now to your governor; will he be pleased with you? Or will he accept you? says Jehovah of hosts" (Mal 1.7–8).

We usually cite these verses when it comes time to put money in the plate. Certainly we should be planning ahead, "purposing in our hearts" what we will give to God, rather than reaching for the leftover change in our pockets. But what about the rest of our "offerings?"

Too many of us give God our leftover time. Rather than planning to pray and study, scheduling time in the week to care for our brothers and sisters in need, and putting our assemblies at the top of our agendas, we wait till we have finished what **we** consider necessary, then look to see if we can give any time and energy to God. Usually it is too late or something else that really cannot be rescheduled takes the last few minutes of our day. If there is time, we are tired, our energy flagging and our concentration poor. No wonder some of the children I have taught in Bible classes treat the concept of a family Bible study as something unheard of. No wonder the adults in Bible classes sit close-mouthed with little to offer to edify their brothers and sisters, or spout out something that even a quick study of scripture would prove to be wrong.

It only makes sense for us to give God our best. God has given us His best too, an only begotten Son, "the firstfruits of them that are asleep" (1 Cor 15.20), as a hope of the resurrection.

God not only expects us to give our first-fruits, he expects us to be one. "Of his own will he brought us forth by the word of truth, that we should be a kind of firstfruits of his creatures" (Jas 1.18). Maybe that is the problem—our lives do not match the concept. Instead, we are the blemished fruit, the tough, small, wormy, and half-rotten. How can we give God anything else when that is all we have to offer? This business of leftover offerings covers far more than the collection plate, far more than we would like to believe.

Turkey leftovers are one thing. They have a place, especially in the lives of those trying to be good stewards of their blessings. But leftovers in my service to God might as well be fed to the dog.

> *Honor Jehovah with your substance, and with the first-fruits of all your increase: So shall your barns be filled with plenty, and your vats shall overflow with new wine.*
>
> Proverbs 3.9–10

45. Southernisms

I understand that the term "Southernism" refers to a trait of language or behavior that is characteristic of the South or Southerners. I have a cookbook, *Cooking Across the South* compiled by Lillian Marshall, which extrapolates that definition to include certain Southern recipes, particularly older recipes. She includes in that list things like hominy, frocking, poke sallet, and tomato gravy. If you are from north of the Mason-Dixon Line, I am sure you are scratching your head at some of those things, wondering just what in the world they are besides strange.

In the same vein, I wondered if we could stretch that idea to something we might call "Christianisms," things a Christian would do that might seem peculiar to someone who isn't one. Like never using what the world now calls "colorful language;" like remaining calm and civil when someone mistreats you, doing, in fact, something nice for him; like not cheating on your taxes; like giving back the change that a cashier overpays you; like paying attention to the speed limit and other laws of the land even if there is not a trooper behind you; like cooking or cleaning house for an invalid; like making time for the worship on Sunday morning and arriving at the ball game late even if those tickets did cost a small fortune; like being careful of the clothing you choose to wear; like choosing not to see certain movies or watch certain television shows; like thinking that spending time with other Christians is far more enjoyable than things like "clubbing"—these are my idea of Christianisms. I am sure you could add more to the list.

In the cookbook, I must admit, are many things I have never heard of, despite being a born and bred Southerner—frocking, for one. You see I came along at a time when the South was starting to change, especially my part of it. Disney changed everything. Orlando used to be a one-horse town instead of the metropolis it has become. I actually learned how to drive in Tampa on what is now I-275. Can you imagine letting a first timer do that? My part of the South has become less "southern" as the years have passed. So, while I had roots in the traditions of the Deep South, I have lost familiarity with many of them.

Wouldn't it be a shame if we got to that point with "Christianisms"? When you read that list I made, did you stop somewhere along the line and say, "Huh? Why would anyone do that?" Have we allowed the "worldisms" to take the place of concepts and behaviors that ought to be second nature to us? Can we even compose a list of things that make us different or have we become assimilated?

Try making a list of the "Christianisms" in your life today. Make sure you can come up with some, and if not, maybe it's time to make a few changes.

Do all things without grumbling or questioning, that you may be blameless and innocent, children of God without blemish in the midst of a crooked and perverse generation, among whom you shine as lights in the world, holding fast to the word of life.

Philippians 2.14–16

46. Dutch Cocoa

I had heard of "Dutch cocoa" for a long time, assuming it was a special kind made in the Netherlands. I finally discovered that "dutch" has nothing to do with its origin. "Dutching" is a process which removes some of the acid from the cocoa, supposedly enhancing its browning ability and making the chocolate flavor more pronounced. I found some a few years ago and proceeded to make all my usual chocolate recipes, expecting them to be transformed into something even more wonderful than before. I was disappointed. Everything turned nearly black, looking and tasting exactly like Oreos. Aha! At least I had discovered that Nabisco uses dutched cocoa to give those iconic cookies their signature flavor and color.

I am afraid that, at least in this area, I remain plebeian and unrefined. I do not want my Mississippi Mud Cake, my Texas Sheet Cake, my Wellesley Fudge Cake, nor even my plain old fudge brownies to taste like Oreos. And the frosting on a chocolate cake should never be darker than the cake—it is just not right somehow.

I find that is the way I feel about a lot of things. Dumplings should be flat, not puffy, waterlogged biscuits; cookies should be chewy or crisp, never cakey; and tea should be sweet, not bitter, while coffee should be black, not sweet.

And in the spiritual arena, Bible classes should be classes. I need to attend with a mindset to learn, not to show off how much I already know. Would we ever allow our children to teach their own classes from their desks? Yet for some reason we think that those old "read a verse and comment" classes are great. The more people talk, the better the class, some say, when often the opposite is true. When one verse is divorced from its context, all sorts of strange concepts arise. The more people talk, the more confused the babes in Christ may become. And really, shouldn't what the teacher has spent hours preparing be far better than anything any of us can come up with off the cuff? Discussion is one thing; allowing the students to teach the class is quite another.

The word "class" necessarily involves hearing something new, or at least challenging. It may mean I have to think deeper thoughts than usual, that I may actually need to go home and study on my own to fully appreciate what I have been told. Yikes! I might actually need to put in a little more effort than sitting on a pew for an hour.

Sermons should be sermons, not Rotary Club talks. Once again that involves the idea of being challenged to be a better person, to change some area of my life, even, perhaps, to admit wrong at least to myself and God. Can't have that, can we? Why, someone might be offended. If no one *ever* goes away offended (in our use of the term, not the Bible's), I think it is a safe bet that a real sermon has never been preached. "Thou art the man," is difficult to say without someone knowing he is being confronted.

So stop expecting Oreos where there should be none. They are fine in their place, usually with a glass of milk at the kitchen table, but don't put them on the menu at a four star restaurant.

We should feel that way whenever anyone tries to insult our intelligence with Bible classes that are not classes and sermons that are not sermons. We should want the pure, unadulterated word of God "in season and out of season," which translates, "whether we want to hear it or not," whether it is easy or not, and we should want to go deeper and deeper, applying it in our lives, finally transforming us into what God would have us be.

*And they read in the book, in the law of God, distinctly; and they
gave the sense, so that they understood the reading. ...And all
the people went their way to eat and to drink, and to send por-
tions and to make great mirth, because they had understood the
words that were declared unto them.*

Nehemiah 8.8, 12

47. The Very Best Pecan Pie

Pecan pie is a staple at our holiday table. I found a great (and easy) recipe years ago and have not changed it a bit, which itself is notable. Yet when I found a recipe recently for "the very best pecan pie," I decided to give it a try. Pecans, sugar, syrup, eggs, butter, and vanilla—how can you mess it up?

I dutifully followed the recipe in every detail. The only real difference was the syrup. "Corn syrup is tasteless," the author said, so she switched to real maple syrup.

"This had better be good," I thought as I shelled out seven dollars for one small bottle.

It wasn't. No, that's not fair. It did not taste awful, but it wasn't pecan pie.

I reread the article. I should have known when I saw the line, "All you can taste are the pecans," referring to the standard recipe using corn syrup. Well, it is called *Pecan* Pie. It is all about the pecans to us Southerners. This magazine was based in New England. What the chef had created was a Maple Nut Pie because suddenly it was all about the maple syrup. You could have added walnuts, hazelnuts, or almonds and not have known the difference. She had completely changed the focus of the pie.

"The Sabbath was made for man, and not man for the Sabbath" (Mark 2.27). Over and over during his ministry, the scribes and Pharisees plagued Jesus with accusations of breaking the Sabbath. Their many rules and regulations, not found in the law, had turned what God designed to be a blessing for man into a burden.

The Sabbath was a day of rest for God's people, while the pagan world worked seven days a week just to survive. It was a day when they could see to their spiritual needs, and renew their relationship with God. It was a day of "holy convocation" (Lev 23.3). The many rigorous—and ridiculous—traditions had made it a day to dread instead.

Jesus reminded them many times that man should be blessed by the Sabbath, that his good should come because of and sometimes even at the expense of the Sabbath. They pulled their oxen out of the ditch. Why shouldn't he heal?

When you change the focus of a law, you often lose the blessing God intended from that law. Staying with the idea of a special day, what about our Lord's Day? Is it necessary to make it inconvenient in order for it to be sincere worship? Yet, I have heard people argue about changing the times of service in exactly that way. If we have many who come from a distance, and the price of gas has become prohibitive, why can't we meet one time for longer instead of two shorter services without being accused of losing our faith?

Can't you hear Jesus' reaction? The Lord's Day is made for man, not man for the Lord's Day. If inconvenience is what makes it true worship, let's meet at 3:00 a.m.

To make another application, each one of us is responsible for how we view our assemblies, for our focus when we meet. If instead of being a blessing it is nothing more than a rule to follow, then I need to change my focus to God's intended one. We are told that our assembling should "provoke one another to love and good works." Too many times all we get is provoked, and that is our own fault. "Let all be done unto edifying," Paul tells those assembled in 1 Corinthians 14.26. You can't edify a person who sits there like a rock, who listens to find fault, or who wishes he were somewhere else.

Don't change the focus of God's laws. He made them to bless us and help us. When we can't find the blessing, it's because we are focused on ourselves, our own bad attitudes and evil motives, instead of on serving a Creator who loves us and blesses us, and on brethren who count on us for encouragement.

For this is the love of God, that we keep his commandments, and his commandments are not grievous.

1 John 5.3

48. Chili Powder

At the end of the garden season, I dry out my hot chili peppers and make chili powder. I have found a good formula, one part chili pepper, two parts ground cumin, one part dried oregano, and two parts garlic powder. The first few times I made it, I used a blend of Anaheim and cayenne peppers. This year Keith shopped for the chili pepper plants and came home with habaneros. If you know anything about the Scoville heat scale, you know that cayennes, while not at the mild end of the scale, are a couple hundred thousand units removed from habaneros which sit at the hottest end.

To make chili powder, you must first dry the chili peppers, then remove the stems and grind them up. A lot of the heat is in the seeds, so I, being a wimp when it comes to hot peppers, shook out the loose seeds as well—habaneros are hot enough as is. I had enough sense to wear latex gloves while handling these babies, but that is where good sense stopped. When I took the lid off the grinder to see if any pieces remained intact, the cloud of chili powder, totally invisible to the naked eye, rose up into my face. How did I know? My nose started running, my lips started burning, and I sneezed nearly a dozen times. I had pepper-maced myself. I am so very glad I had reading glasses on. I do not know what might have happened to these poor eyes! I know people who don't even use gloves to work with hot peppers, but next time I will reach for a gas mask!

Sin and conscience work the same way. Especially nowadays when sophistication is judged by how little one allows sinful behavior to shock him, we have a tendency to think we can sin indiscriminately and feel just fine about ourselves afterwards. What was it Paul said about the idolatrous pagans? "For when Gentiles who do not have the law, by nature do what the law requires, they are a law to themselves even though they do not have the law. They show that the law of God is written on their hearts, while their conscience also bears witness, and their conflicting thoughts either accuse or even excuse themselves" (Rom 2.14–15). You can't get away from your conscience no matter how sophisticated you think you are.

The scriptures are littered with people who suffered pangs of conscience. Adam and Eve hid themselves after they had sinned. The brothers of Joseph twice confessed their sin against their brother, attributing all the bad things that happened in Egypt with the hostile "Egyptian" ruler as their just recompense. Pharaoh, of all people, said to Moses and Aaron, "This time I have sinned. The Lord is in the right, and I and my people are in the wrong" (Exod 9.27). David sinned more than the once we often focus on. His "heart smote him" after he numbered the people in 2 Samuel 24 and his psalms of repentance after the sin against Bathsheba and Uriah abound with overwhelming guilt.

Herod was so wrought with guilt after killing John that he thought Jesus was John coming back from the dead. Peter's denial caused him to "weep bitterly," while Judas's betrayal led to suicide. Even Paul, a man who surely knew he was forgiven, called himself "the chiefest of sinners" to the end of his life.

And we think we can get away with sin and have it not affect us? Guilt is like that burning chili pepper cloud. You can't see it, but your conscience will still feel its effects, and if you don't deal with it, you will lead a miserable life—at least until you burn that conscience out as if you had "branded it with a hot iron" (1 Tim 4.2).

Do you know how to get rid of the pain of burning chili peppers? Dairy products. If you forget your gloves and those oils get under your nails or in a nick or cut, soak your hands in milk. That is also why there is usually a dollop of sour cream on most Mexican dishes.

Do you know how to get rid of the pain of a burning conscience? Soak it in the blood of Christ. It works wonders.

> *For if the blood of goats and bulls and the ashes of a heifer sprinkling them that have been defiled sanctify unto the cleanness of the flesh, how much more shall the blood of Christ who through the eternal Spirit offered himself without blemish unto God, cleanse your conscience from dead works to serve the living God?*
>
> Hebrews 9.13–14

49. Cultured Buttermilk

In the old days buttermilk was simply the liquid left over after churning butter. It was thin and watery, and not sour at all, unless you allowed your cream to "ripen" a few days before churning, something high end butter makers still do today.

Nowadays buttermilk is skim milk to which cultures have been added to develop flavor and to thicken consistency. Buttermilk has its place in the baker's refrigerator. It adds tang and helps the rise, especially when used with baking soda. You will have the highest and fluffiest biscuits and pancakes you ever made.

The word "culture" has several meanings. A culture can be a special nutrient in which things are grown, usually in laboratories. In agriculture it can refer to tillage to prepare the land for planting. It can apply to a specific community of people and their shared beliefs and customs, and also the things they produce like art, music, and literature. Can you see in all these cases a relationship to growth and improvement? In the kitchen it certainly produces better baked goods. But culture can be negative as well. The culture of Sodom and Gomorrah produced a sinful lifestyle that led to its destruction.

Ruth understood the effects of a culture. This brave young widow was willing to leave behind her culture and embrace another just so she could worship Jehovah. In her world, no matter the culture, widows could look forward to only two things—either a new husband to support her, or poverty for the rest of her life. "Orphans and widows" were the symbol of helplessness throughout the scriptures. Ruth's best bet for a happy and prosperous life was to stay in her homeland among her own people and find that new husband.

But something was more important to her than her comfort zone, as we so often call it. She completely changed her culture. She left home for a place where she had to learn a new language, new customs and traditions, and new laws. She left her family and her friends for a people not known for accepting strangers with open arms. Why do you think the law is full of reminders to take care of "strangers and sojourners?" We know the end of the story, but Ruth didn't. She had nothing to look forward to but a life of hard work and poverty, dependent upon whether or not these new people she was willing to claim as her own followed the laws God set up to support widows. I think it is obvious that even if they had not, her conversion was to Jehovah, not them, and she would have continued on anyway.

How about us? Do we have the strength to give up our culture? Language, fashion, music, literature, entertainment, and what passes as art these days is often completely opposed to the righteousness God expects of his people. Can you give it up?

I find it helps to think of it like this: I am not giving up my culture to stand alone. I am giving up one culture for another. Our citizenship is in Heaven, Paul reminds us in Philippians 3.20. Just as Ruth was willing to embrace a new culture, we should too, and in that embracing we find support from those who are just like us. We are no longer standing alone against the crowd.

Which culture do you live in this morning?

But Ruth said, "Do not urge me to leave you or to return from following you. For where you go I will go, and where you lodge I will lodge. Your people shall be my people, and your God my God. Where you die I will die, and there will I be buried. May the LORD do so to me and more also if anything but death parts me from you."

Ruth 1.16–17

50. Shortbread

I love shortbread—real butter, flour, sugar, a pinch of salt, and a little good vanilla. Pat it in a pan and bake it. With black coffee, or hot chocolate, or hot tea, or even good old Southern sweet tea to wash it down, I am happy.

Another thing I like about shortbread is its versatility. You can pat it in a round cake pan and cut it into wedges after it is baked. You can pat it into an oblong pan and cut the finished cookies into fingers, triangles, or squares. You can roll out the dough and cut it into shapes before baking. You can stamp an emblem on it.

Add some chopped toasted pecans and you have pecan shortbread. Roll those into balls, and roll the baked cookies in powdered sugar and you have pecan sandies.

Exchange almond paste for some of the butter. Leave out the vanilla and add almond extract; brush the dough with egg white and sprinkle with sparkling sugar and sliced almonds. Suddenly your simple shortbread is almond shortbread.

Add the grated zest of a lemon instead of vanilla. Slather the cooked bars with a glaze made of the same lemon's juice and some powdered sugar—iced lemon shortbread bars. (Warning: this is an adult cookie; kids are not crazy about it.)

Cut your plain old shortbread into fingers. Then, after baking and cooling, dip one end into melted semi-sweet or bittersweet chocolate. Leave some plain chocolate. Dip others in chopped nuts before the chocolate sets. Plain shortbread has suddenly become elegant.

You can even use shortbread dough as the base for a layered dessert. Just bake it and cool it first, enough to cover a 9"X13" pan. Add chopped nuts or not before baking as you please. The layers can be three or four of your choosing—various flavors and mixings of pudding, peanut butter, cream cheese, powdered sugar, fruit pie fillings, drained crushed pineapple, sweetened whipped cream, chopped nuts, toasted coconut, chopped chocolate bars, whatever you can imagine. Chill and cut into layered squares, either light or rich, depending on your choices. And it all started with a base of butter, flour, sugar, and vanilla.

Any time I hear someone say the Bible is no longer relevant, I think of shortbread. It doesn't matter for which of life's situations you need guidance, God's word contains something to help you. Not only does it include the principles of marriage, but several real life examples as well—everything from good, sound marriages to marriages dealing with unfaithfulness and abuse. The same is true with childrearing. We are not stuck with abstract ideas like "raise your children in the nurture and admonition of the Lord." We have examples of parents who made a mess of things—favoritism, lack of discipline, provocation, poor teaching. We have parents who loved too much and in the wrong ways. And we have the results of all those mistakes in heartbreaking detail.

We have stories of neighbors who couldn't get along and how they settled things. We have stories of servants (think "employees") who served well, and those who didn't, and what made the difference. We have stories of good masters (employers) and bad. We have stories of those who handled power well and those who did not. And if you can't find exactly the same circumstances you need help with, "As you would that men should do unto you, do you also unto them," covers a whole lot of territory, including email and cell phone etiquette.

Just as shortbread can fit any situation from a children's lunch to a family meal to an elegant party, God's word works no matter what situation you find yourself in. Keep a close eye out and I think you will find that people who think the Bible is irrelevant simply don't want to follow its guidelines. It isn't that God says nothing about their situation; it's that they don't like His solution.

But that is nothing new either. Ahab, one of the wickedest kings in Israel's history, said of the prophet Micaiah, "I don't like him because he never says anything good about me." There was a way to fix that; Ahab just didn't like the remedy.

God does not leave his children without guidance in every situation they might encounter. It is up to us to find that guidance and obey it.

> *The works of his hands are faithful and just; all his precepts are trustworthy; They are established forever and ever, to be performed with faithfulness and uprightness.*

> Psalm 111.7–8

51. Fudge

During the holidays I usually try to make a batch of chocolate fudge. I say "try" because I usually fail. Peanut butter fudge I have down. Nineteen out of 20 times it will turn out right, but not the chocolate variety. I am talking about real fudge, not the newer recipes that add things like marshmallow crème, and wind up changing the texture just so it won't flop on you. If it shines, it isn't fudge; if it's soft, it isn't fudge; if it's grainy, it isn't fudge; if it must be kept refrigerated, it isn't fudge. Real fudge is matte to the eye, firm to the touch, creamy in your mouth, and sits just fine on the countertop without changing consistency.

So a couple of years ago I found a recipe for foolproof fudge in a cooking magazine that I ordinarily trust implicitly. I made their recipe, and indeed it did just fine, but it was shiny, it was soft, it had to be stored in the refrigerator. It wasn't fudge, and I was disappointed beyond measure. However, in the article accompanying the recipe, the author stated that fudge is a tricky thing. If the temperature and humidity are not just right, if your ingredients have sucked up too much moisture from the kitchen atmosphere any time recently, if your candy thermometer is just a degree or two off, your fudge will not "fudge." He went on to say that even seasoned professionals feel frustrated when trying to make this unreasonably difficult recipe. While I am sorry those folks feel that way, it certainly made me feel a lot better. It helped explain my one in ten record of success over the years.

Aren't we glad salvation is not so difficult? Just follow a few simple directions and suddenly you have a relationship that will help you in the trials of this life, and lead you to the joys of the next, the sweetest of treats anyone could possibly enjoy. Why is it that some people feel so obligated to make it more difficult?

My brother-in-law was nearly run out of a church on a rail once because, using the Philippian jailor of Acts 16 as an example, he dared to say that there really is not all that much we have to know before we submit to baptism. Oh no, he was told, we must know all about the plan of God through the ages, about the true nature of the first century church, about the false teachings on salvation and how to combat them, about the "correct" definitions of faith, baptism, and grace, among other things.

Just what was it Philip asked that Ethiopian proselyte when he wanted to be baptized? "If you believe with all your heart, you may, and he said, I believe that Jesus Christ is the Son of God" (Acts 8.37). Funny that Philip never gave him a list of things to memorize and recite before he was allowed in the water. Isn't it wonderful—and amazing!—that our Lord will accept our obedient faith the moment we realize our need for Him?

Yes, there are many things we must all learn. All these years after my baptism there are still many more. That's what the rest of your life is for; that's why Peter said to "grow in the grace and knowledge of the Lord and Savior Jesus Christ" (2 Pet 3.18). We never finish that part. Maybe the problem is, we make this arbitrary list and think once we know it, we *are* finished. Just who made the list in the first place, if God didn't?

One of Satan's most powerful tools is frustration and hopelessness. Let's not help him do his work by making salvation so difficult that people give up before they even get the chance to start.

And [the jailor] *called for lights and sprang in, and trembling for fear, fell down before Paul and Silas and brought them out and said, Sirs, what must I do to be saved? And they said, Believe on the Lord Jesus and you shall be saved, you and your house; and they spoke the word of the Lord unto him with all that were in his house, and he took them* **the same hour of the night** *and washed their stripes and was baptized, he and all his immediately.*

Acts 16.29–33

52. The Tablecloth

My grandmother crocheted a lace tablecloth for me many years ago. She was quite a lady, my grandmother. She was widowed in her forties, left behind with two of her five children still at home. She met the bills by doing seasonal work in the citrus packing sheds of central Florida, standing on her feet 10–12 hours a day, six days a week in season, and then working in a drugstore, a job she walked to and from for nearly 30 years. She delivered prescriptions, worked the check-out, even made sodas at the fountain.

It was a small town and once, a woman whom my grandmother knew was not married, came in looking for some form of birth control. My grandmother told her, "No! Go home and behave yourself like a decent woman should." No, she did not lose her job over that. She merely said what every other person there wished they had the nerve to say back in those days. She lived long enough to see the shame of our society that no one thinks it needs saying any more.

As to my tablecloth, most people would look at it and think it was imperfect. She crocheted with what was labeled "ivory" thread, but she could never afford to buy enough at once to do the whole piece. So after she cashed her paycheck, she went to the store and bought as much as her budget would allow that week and worked on it. The next week, she went back and did the same, always buying the same brand labeled "ivory." Funny thing about those companies, though—when the lot changes, sometimes the color does too, sometimes only a little, but sometimes "ivory" becomes more of a vanilla or even crème caramel. The intricately crocheted squares in my tablecloth are not all the same color, even though the thread company said they were.

Some people probably look at it and wonder what went wrong. All they see is mismatched colors. What I see is a grandmother's love, a grandmother who had very little, but who wanted to do something special for her oldest grandchild. I revel in those mismatched squares because I know my grandmother thought of me every week for a long time, spent the precious little she had to try to do something nice, and, as far as I am concerned, succeeded far beyond her wildest dreams.

If it were your grandmother, you would think the same I am sure. So why is it we think Almighty God cannot take our imperfections and make us into great men and women of faith? Why is it we beat ourselves to death when we make a mistake, even one we repent of and do our best to correct? Do we not yet understand grace? Are we so arrogant that we think we don't have to forgive ourselves even though God does? Yes we should understand the enormity of our sin, repenting in godly sorrow, over and over, even as David did, but prolonged groveling in the pit of unworthiness can be more about self-pity and lacking faith in God to do what he promised than it is about humility. The longer we indulge in it, the less we are doing for the Lord, and Satan is just as pleased as if we had gone on sinning. Either way helps him out.

The next time you look into a mirror and see only your faults, remember my tablecloth. When you give God all you have, he can make you into something beautiful too.

And God is able to make all grace abound unto you, that you, always having all sufficiency in everything, may abound unto every good work.

2 Corinthians 9.8

Little Blue Almonds

In the early 1950s, a little girl was born in a small town hospital which sat almost in the middle of a Florida orange grove. Six pounds, eight ounces, curly black hair, and blue eyes.

About those eyes—perfect little blue almonds, but something just a little different about them. An imprudent woman once asked her mother, "Why are her eyes slanted?" A little offended and a lot nonplussed, she answered, "Because her father was in Korea when she was born," which was all that question deserved.

By the time she was four, it had become apparent that those eyes did indeed have a problem. She kept pulling her little black rocking chair closer and closer to the walnut console television set till she sat not more than a foot from it, leaning forward, peering into the screen. So her parents made an appointment and, sure enough, she had severe hyperopia—farsightedness, "the worst case I've seen short of blindness," the doctor said.

The first pair of thick glasses hung over the frames a good half inch, and the heavy glasses constantly slid down her nose. But for the first time in her short life, she saw an ant crawling across the sidewalk.

Suddenly other children became a real part of her life. Instead of voices swimming around dimly perceived shapes, they developed eyes, noses, and mouths. She could actually play with them. But her vision was now a long narrow tunnel. She couldn't see what lay at her feet or stood off to the side or hovered above her head. So playing meant tripping and falling every time she ran across the playground. It meant every ball she ever tried to play with hit her squarely in the face before she saw it coming—volleyballs, softballs, kickballs, tetherballs. And dodgeballs? She was easy prey. It became much safer to sit in her room and read, and then, amazingly enough, to play the piano, her fingers crawling across the smooth, cool black and white keys at the bottom of her narrow tunnel.

Those children she could now see could see her too, and, as children are wont to be, were frank about how she looked. Her little almonds, hazel now, had become big protruding bug eyes behind the strong lenses. Adults, too, their words swarming over her head like biting flies, said things like, "It's a shame she has to wear those Big Ugly Glasses." That's how she heard it— capital Big, and *very* capital Ugly. Those big, ugly glasses meant she could function; they were a blessing. Still, it was easier on both body and heart to sit alone in the tunnel. Ultimately, she became convinced that since she could see no one except those right in front of her, they couldn't see her either, and it was much better that way.

By the age of 13, a couple of family moves meant she was on her third doctor. She now wore bifocals as her vision had continued to deteriorate. This older doctor had a new young associate, a graduate of the University of Chicago, who had ideas he wanted to try with this patient. "If we don't do something," he said, "you will simply continue to get worse, and there's really not much further to go."

Contact lenses had just become available a few years before—the hard kind, the uncomfortable kind, the ones that are neither soft nor gas permeable. Her eyeballs were steep, the corneas shaped like the end of a corrugated football and the prescription would be +17.25. Contacts would never fit her, and even if he could somehow manage it, they would be incredibly uncomfortable. "You will have to *want* to do this," he told the scared 14 year old, "or you won't be able to. It's as simple as that."

So she set her mind to it, and on that hot June day when those contact lenses arrived, she put them on. Yes, they hurt.

Yes, she blinked constantly, her eyes watering from the sensation of *something* being in them. For the whole day she sat in a room in his office, learning how to put them in and take them out, wearing them ten minutes, then taking them out for twenty to give her eyes a break, over and over and over.

At noon, the kind doctor reached into his pocket and pulled out change. "Go for a walk," he said, "and see how you like them outside. Buy yourself a soda. Come back in 30 minutes."

So she did, and that hooked her. She could see more than the tunnel in front of her for the first time in her life. The sensation of light and movement all around her, especially in the busy downtown traffic, was dizzying and nearly overwhelming. But she didn't trip over the curbs or step into anything disgusting someone ahead of her had dropped. She saw a man hurrying up the sidewalk on her right and stepped out of his way. When she looked down to count the change for the drink at the drug store, she barely had to tilt her head at all. It was amazing.

So she persevered through that first painful day and the painful weeks that followed, on a schedule of two hours on and two hours off, then four on and two off, then six, then eight, until, at the end of the summer she was able to wear them all day, which by college years was sometimes as long as 20 hours. They could only correct her vision to 20/40 and the lenses never did sit quite right on her corneas, but she saw so much more it was as if she were seeing perfectly.

A Race Against Time

The routine of life continued on. Contact lenses improved and she was able to wear the new gas permeables as soon as they became available. Her doctor retired and, forced to find another, she once again became aware of how special those eyes were. In one place she lived, the doctor she found greeted her with, "You're the kind of patient I wish had never walked into my office." So she never did again.

Over and over she was told how lucky she was. "You should

never have gotten this far." "You should have been blind by 20." "These are extremely rare eyes." "This is the worst case I have ever treated." "Your old doctor was a genius. These contacts should *not* work on eyes like yours, but somehow they do." Still she continued to live her life as if it were all normal. It *was* normal to her; she had never known anything else.

Then without warning, just three weeks after her fiftieth birthday, her latest doctor walked into the office carrying a clipboard and pen, as well as her chart. It was supposed to be a regular, semi-annual check-up, something she had done nearly a hundred times, but it wasn't. The day was Halloween, and instead of a treat, she got a trick.

He began to draw an eyeball, a funny looking squashed-up thing, not at all like the big plastic models the doctors all have standing on their desks or printed on the posters on their walls. He explained to her exactly what was wrong with her eyes. She was born not just hyperopic, but aphakic, with a severe case of nanophthalmus, and a defect called anatomical narrow angle. The anterior chamber of her eye, the space between the iris and the cornea, was shrinking. The angles, which were already narrow, were closing up and the eye could no longer drain properly. Pressure was already rising. An angle closure attack would occur if something were not done. And with that he shut up her chart and sent her on to the first of two world famous eye surgeons.

The first surgery was relatively easy. The doctor drilled holes into each eye with a laser to act as a kind of release valve to lower the rising pressure. It worked for a year, but the lens in the eye thickens with age, and hers thickening in an eyeball just over half the size of a normal one, created an insurmountable problem. The hyperopia did not help. Even if they took out her natural lens and replaced it, they would need to piggy-back two new lenses into her eye to give her any sort of decent vision at all. There was simply no room for two lenses in that tiny eyeball. It was either go blind from an angle closure attack or be blind from having no lens in the eye.

Providence stepped in. This world famous doctor just happened to have met another world famous doctor at a conference halfway around the world, who just happened to know an inventor in Germany who just weeks before had perfected a new lens—one made with prisms so that more power could be crammed into a thinner lens. She packed her bags and traveled a thousand miles to see this second surgeon, and yes, he thought he could help. But this intra-ocular lens was not yet approved in the United States. They would have to apply for a compassionate waiver, a one time deal for one patient only. She would have to "sign her life away," they said.

It was already March, two months after the original decision. How long would the approval process take? She had possibly only a few weeks until the angle closure attack occurred, and then it would be too late. By the first of May, the second doctor had phoned the FDA to find out what was taking so long. They had had a change in leadership he was told, and papers sat piling up on his desk until the new head of the department could get his bearings and begin to go through them—in order as received.

Then on June 1, the little girl, who had somehow become a middle-aged woman, married 30 years with two grown sons, began seeing circles and starbursts far worse than anything her contact lenses had ever caused before. The right eye ached deep in the socket, and nausea swept over her like a wave. An angle closure attack, her local world famous doctor said. After 18 hours it stopped. Why? The doctors do not know—but she does.

Twelve days later, she lay on an operating table keeping a death-grip on her gown beneath stiff, white sheets that covered her head to toe, watching the blue kaleidoscope light show as the second surgeon in a city a thousand miles from her family, cut into her eye and inserted the fancy new German lens. She had to be awake for the surgery, so she could answer questions, but that meant she could hear all too well. Just a little while into the procedure the doctor quietly said,

"We have angle closure." Somehow—she knew how—they had made it just in time.

Complications set in the next day, but within a week, she was cleared to go home. Six months later, surgery saved the second eye. No one knew how long it would last, just "awhile."

A year later, the left eye headed south again. This time the procedure called for, a trabeculectomy and installation of an ophthalmic shunt, was the specialty of her local man, and yet another scary surgery ensued. This one had complications that lasted two full months with frantic, almost daily procedures to resolve them, and then the whole thing had to be repeated seven months later, but once again the eyes were still working—not as well as before, but, "It's not about improving your vision," the doctor said. "It's about saving it." Funny how perspective can turn disappointment into joy.

How long will it last this time? It has already gone far longer than anyone expected. The year ahead may bring challenges far worse than any that have gone before. But the little girl has grown up and come out of her tunnel. She has come to understand that while the circumstances of life may shape that life, they must not determine it. The truly spiritual mind views physical life as a tool in God's great plan of salvation, one that must be wielded in whatever way possible at whatever cost. She has learned that He continues to expect whatever service she can offer, not simply as long as she has sight, but until faith has become sight.

So we do not lose heart. Though our outer self is wasting away, our inner self is being renewed day by day. For this light momentary affliction is preparing for us an eternal weight of glory beyond all comparison, as we look not to the things that are seen but to the things that are unseen. For the things that are seen are transient, but the things that are unseen are eternal.

2 Corinthians 4.16–18

Also by Dene Ward

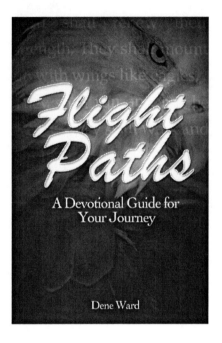

Flight Paths
A Devotional Guide for your Journey

When encroaching blindness took her music teaching career away, Dene Ward turned her attention to writing. What began as e-mail devotions to some friends grew into a list of hundreds of subscribers. Three hundred sixty-six of those devotions have been assembled to form this daily devotional. Follow her through a year of camping, bird-watching, medical procedures, piano lessons, memories, and more as she uses daily life as a springboard to thought-provoking and character-challenging messages of endurance and faith. 475 pages. $18.99 (PB)

Built By the Lord: A Study of the Family
Edwin Crozier

A biblical and challenging look at the Lord-built home. *Built by the Lord* answers questions about the purpose of the Lord-built home, the roles in the Lord-built home, the goals of the Lord-built home, the habits a Lord-built home maintains, and how the Lord-built home interacts with the Lord's family. Each chapter comes packed with Biblically-based teaching, challenging personal responses, points for further meditation, and prayer to seed your own prayer life inviting God to build your home. 226 pages. $13.99 (PB)

A Worthy Woman (revised edition)
Darlene Craig

Proverbs 31 presents a strong, joyful woman of wisdom, integrity, devotion, talent, industry, compassion, faith and influence. Darlene uses the example of the ideal woman to strengthen and encourage real women of all ages to further realize their "far above rubies" value as they joyfully strive to positively impact the lives of their families and others. 194 pages. $11.99 (PB)

The Slave of Christ
Seth Parr

Immerse yourself in a place where sacrifice is reasonable, love and action are sensible, victory is guaranteed, and evangelism explodes. While the sacrifice of Jesus opens the door for us to Heaven, we must work to be conformed into His very image. In The Slave of Christ, uncover what biblical service means and how it can change your life. Energize your spiritual walk and awaken the servant within. 96 pages. $8.99 (PB)

Hello, I'm Your Bible
Jason Hardin

A practical guide to understanding and applying
God's word of truth. Whether you've just been in-
troduced to the Bible, you'd like to get reacquainted
with the Scriptures, or you're looking to grow in
your ability to help others in their walk of faith,
Hello, I'm Your Bible can guide you into a deeper relationship with the God behind the living and active word. 156 pages. $9.99 (PB)

Churches of the New Testament
Ethan Longhenry

Have you ever wondered what it would be like to be
a Christian in the first century? What would it be
like to meet with the church in Philippi or Ephesus?
What would go on in their assemblies? Churches
of the New Testament explores the world of first
century Christianity by examining what Scripture
reveals about the local churches of God's people. It
examines background information about the geog-
raphy and history of each city, as well as whatever
is known about the founding of the church there.

This book also considers what happened to the church after the first century. Centuries may separate us from the churches of the New Testament,
but their examples, instruction, commendation, and rebukes can teach us
today. 150 pages. $9.99 (PB)

*For a full listing of DeWard Publishing
Company books, visit our website:*

www.deward.com

CPSIA information can be obtained at www.ICGtesting.com
Printed in the USA
BVOW02s1906200813

329023BV00001B/5/P

9 781936 341337